CRAVINGS

CONTENTS

 *Contents*

Every human being is the author of his own health.

—THE BUDDHA

This book is dedicated to:

Dr. Richard Ash, naturopath and healer

William Banting, mortician to English royalty, who wrote the first true diet book, Letter on Corpulence, *in 1864 (still in print)*

Princess Diana, who spoke out publicly about her bulimia

Bill Wilson and Dr. Bob Smith, who gave us the answers to addiction

Father Ed Dowling, who told Bill Wilson and Dr. Bob Smith that he had the same problems with food that they had with alcohol

Karen Carpenter, who died of her eating disorder long before most people knew there was such a thing

The material in this book is supplied for informational purposes only and is not meant to take the place of a doctor's advice. Before embarking on any regimen of diet and exercise you should first consult your own physician.

All rights reserved. Published in the United States by Nan A. Talese/Doubleday, a division of Penguin Random House LLC, New York, and distributed in Canada by Random House of Canada, a division of Penguin Random House Canada Limited, Toronto.

www.nanatalese.com

Book design by Pei Loi Koay
Jacket design by Emily Mahon
Back jacket photograph © 2015 by Brad Trent

LIBRARY OF CONGRESS CATALOGING-IN-PUBLICATION DATA
Names: Collins, Judy, 1939– author.
Title: Cravings : how I conquered food / Judy Collins.
Description: New York : Nan A. Talese, 2017. | Includes bibliographical references.
Identifiers: LCCN 2016009368 (print) | LCCN 2016026321 (ebook) | ISBN 9780385541312 (hardcover) | ISBN 9780385541329 (ebook)
Subjects: LCSH: Collins, Judy, 1939– Health. | Bulimia—Patients—United States—Biography. | Compulsive eating—United States—Biography. | Eating disorders—Patients—United States—Biography. | Singers—United States—Biography. |
BISAC: BIOGRAPHY & AUTOBIOGRAPHY / Personal Memoirs. | BIOGRAPHY & AUTOBIOGRAPHY / Entertainment & Performing Arts. | PSYCHOLOGY / Psychopathology / Addiction.
Classification: LCC RC552.B84 C65 2017 (print) | LCC RC552.B84 (ebook) | DDC 616.85/2630092 [B] —DC23
LC record available at https://lccn.loc.gov/2016009368

MANUFACTURED IN THE UNITED STATES OF AMERICA

1 3 5 7 9 10 8 6 4 2

First Edition

CRAVINGS

. . .

HOW I CONQUERED FOOD

Judy Collins

NAN A. TALESE | DOUBLEDAY

NEW YORK LONDON TORONTO

SYDNEY AUCKLAND

CRAVINGS

The Source of the Trouble

Do not cut the wings of your dreams, for they are the
heartbeat and the freedom of your soul.

—FLAVIA

Cravings is a memoir of my long struggle with an eating
disorder. It is also the story of a search for a spiritual solution to my problems with food. As an active, working
alcoholic with an eating disorder, I yearned for serenity and was tormented for much of my life by longings,
addictions, and painful crises over food: bingeing, bulimia, weight loss and gain. I was determined from an early
age that I would *never* get fat. I would rather die.

That was the driving idea behind all the trouble. From
the beginning I wanted to look good. Like a jockey who
has to get on that horse, like the dancer who must get
into the tutu, like the gymnast who has to fly up to the

bar, I would do anything to lose the few pounds that would, as I saw it, disqualify me from the games.

In music I had always found the spiritual solace I longed for. In my addictions I lived in a spiritual desert and had to find water and sustenance, the spark of inspiration and some solution that would end the drama of diets, pills, plans, doctors, extreme answers, and mutilating consequences. This is the story of the mountains I have climbed and the demons I have encountered, as well as many of the diet gurus I have come to know on the path to recovery. The book is the story of finally filling the black hole in my soul that comes with untreated food addiction.

Since my first attempt to diet in the early 1960s—a combination of alcohol and Atkins—trying to tame the beast that will always live inside my skin, I have tried dozens of diets and methods to control and manipulate my weight, and to shed the pounds and the shame that were brought about by the illness of compulsive overeating. After many decades of searching, I finally found the answer—or I should say I was given the courage to surrender to what I knew worked best—which has brought me peace of mind, a clean food plan, years of remaining at the same weight, and a glow of joy and health. The discovery of a solution to my problem has prompted the desire to share what I have learned.

There are no coincidences—I found a book by Louise

Foxcroft in 2012 that delved into the diet habits of people over the centuries. I have always been an activist and have talked about many of the troubling secrets from my childhood and adolescence. (Lena Dunham may have had something to do with this sudden impulse to tell more of what was buried deep in my psyche, what I never talked about in depth, even to many therapists through the years, since her show, *Girls,* is inspiring young men and women to own their issues.) I have spoken out about my alcoholism, and about the suicide of my only child, and what it is like to be a survivor of my attempt on my own life at fourteen. It seemed time to tell my story, and to encourage those who suffer from the same problems that there is another way through the dark night of the soul of compulsive overeating. So how did I stop?

I have a condition that I have learned is an illness, like alcoholism, like other addictions. It is not a moral failing, as alcoholism is not a moral failing, but a true disease. It is incurable unless I find a solution on a daily basis. I am going to die from this illness or one of its many side effects if I do not take care of it one day at a time, with a balanced food plan free of the foods that could kill me—sugar, grains, flour, wheat, corn, and many foods to which I am allergic (most of which are in alcohol, strangely enough)—and that could cause anyone with these allergies to become bulimic, anorexic, or overweight; bring on feelings of fear and self-loathing;

and cause diabetes, high blood pressure, and heart disease. What other reasons could I possibly have for finding a solution to this simple problem?

In order to keep on this path I must have more than a diet—any diet—I must have a life plan, one that will work every day. This is not to say that any of the diets I have been on or talk about are at fault—they are all good and work if you follow them. They are all the result of someone wanting or needing to lose weight and, in that pursuit, telling us how to remove the offending foods from our lives.

I have failed most of these diets; they did not fail me.

No matter how smart and dedicated the food writers and doctors who showed me what to eat were, I failed because I had to have the help of whatever you want to call it—God, a Power greater than myself. In the Anonymous programs they call this the "group conscience." Churches all over the world have helped those in need and intend to be of service. Most of us have struggled in spite of these religious organizations and communities. We must find another kind of church for food addiction, and for most of us, that is an inward journey, perhaps a combination of all the universal ideals of the founders of churches, driven by their original concepts of spiritual power.

We must each find our own way.

I am writing from my own experience, from sixty years of struggling to find the solution. What I have to share may not be the only answer to the problems of compulsive eating or the frustration, agony, and health problems that result from eating the wrong kind of food over a lifetime. But I have tried most diets and can tell you that if my solution worked for me, it might work for you. None of us knows what our use-by date might be. In order to live happy, healthy, fat- and despair-free lives, we must find something that works one day at a time.

I have been sober for thirty-eight years now, and I do not have to drink alcohol. But three times a day I still have to face food. How to do that has been my lifelong struggle. The fight is over and I want to share how that happened.

I always worked hard at controlling what I thought of as my shameful inclinations. These overpowering urges to eat and drink more than the other children at the party meant I must be a bad girl, not able to behave like the others, to have one slice, one drink, one piece of choco-late was not something I could ever do. I was not able to bring the world into line with my desires, my idea of who and how I should be.

In my struggle with food it was always my goal to look thinner—to get into my clothes, to feel free and easy when I walked away from or ran toward someone. Since I would rather be dead than fat, how would I deal with food? I have thrown up in the bathrooms of a thousand restaurants; bought bags and boxes of sweets and eaten them at one sitting; fought my way through more than thirty years of therapists and doctors who tried to help me; nearly ruined my voice with purging; taken laxatives for years on end; done colonics and starvation cleanses. I have bounced from doctor to doctor, taken pills to shed the weight and dieted to keep it off, then broken the diet and put back every pound, misery piling on misery. In an effort to control my eating I have been to health farms and subjected myself to long fasts. I have read all the best-selling books—from Adelle Davis's *Let's Get Well* to *Sugar Blues,* William Dufty's compendium of the dangers of sugar; and from *Eat to Live* to *The Conscious Cleanse.* I have gone on every diet I could find, in every decade. I have taken all the little pills, uppers and downers prescribed by a diet doctor in New York City. I have been on Dr. Lynn's liquid diet, eaten only celery, melons, and other vegetables that supposedly burn more calories than they contain.

And then I was back in the game, gaining weight, feeling heartbroken and deprived, despairing and suicidal, insane with the compulsions I had no way of controlling. I always knew I needed clear-cut boundaries with my food, but for decades I couldn't find a long-term solution, and the advice I was given provided only brief, fleeting, relief.

I am not a medical doctor, just a survivor who has learned more in my lifetime about eating disorders than most doctors.

Suicide would be the answer for me if I did not have

another answer. For me, that solution has been a combination of information and a set of spiritual practices—attention to the breath, perhaps just remaining in one place at a time; being quiet; the river rolling by, my eye on the sky; my mind calmed by music, or prayer, or loving friends who can share this journey with me and tell me all will be revealed, all will be well. All is well.

When I was controlled by food, my soul shrank and my fear grew. When I was abstinent, my soul grew and my body shrank. When I was in the depths of my eating disorder, not only was I obsessed with food but my mind never stopped. The chatter, the talk, the back and forth, the internal argument was never-ending. The peace of mind, quiet, and serenity that I prayed for from the depths of my illness came with surrender. It is something for which I am eternally grateful.

I once was telling a seriously overweight friend that one of our mutual friends had died of alcoholism, literally drinking himself to death.

"Thank God I never got into that!" she said, congratulating herself. She is a very bright woman, and yet she was unable to associate her own problem—morbid obesity—with the illness of addiction to alcohol that had killed our friend.

Compulsive overeating, anorexia, bulimia, and bouncing from one insane diet to another are all in the same family of illness. Like alcoholism, they are coming to be understood as addictions. The things I didn't know—

the "cloud of unknowing," as some religious people put it—have come to be my teacher, my leveler, my answer, my relief. Not knowing has finally led to a solution. My solution. It could be yours, who knows.

I love solutions. In my search for sanity about food I had to find a way to surrender my old ideas and find new ones that work.

I talk about allergies, but the truth is that if you are overweight; have a problem with bulimia, anorexia, bingeing, or starving; or if you worry about what you are going to eat all the time; or are going on different diets every few weeks, you probably have a serious issue with food and it may be helpful to turn yourself over to a program that is encouraging, sustaining, and friendly and offers the right foods and the right support. The program I have found is supported by a fellowship of people who do what I do and love to talk about it, on the phone, in person, at meetings of like-minded people, and just about anywhere you bring them together. It is like having a support group if you have cancer. And an eating disorder is a serious illness that must be addressed 24-7, 365 days a year, just like other life-threatening ill-nesses. There is really very little difference, except that many people understand the need for support for getting through cancer better than they understand it for get-ting through an eating disorder or other addiction. When someone is suffering from a disease such as cancer, they get sympathy and support. It is time we see food addiction and compulsive eating as just as dangerous, just as painful, and in many cases just as devastating as many other diseases.

The depth of the problem is partly reflected in how many books there are out there offering solutions to obesity, addiction, diabetes, high blood pressure, and heart disease. And the answer is that most of these illnesses can and should be largely addressed with diet change. In fact, eventually they must be in order for us to achieve total health. The faces of eating disorders are all around us today, hard to miss and potentially life-threatening for many of us. The food issues in our culture threaten to destroy our health-care infrastructure and thwart our ability to heal the plague of obesity.

I did not know when I was young that the illness of compulsive eating is in the mind as well as the body. I was never notably heavy, but I have gained and lost at least a thousand pounds in my struggle to pare down and keep the weight off, while I tried to eat "normally." The struggle has been exhausting and has created terror and chaos in my life, from fasting to bulimia, from compulsive exercise to restricting food, from broken promises to loss of bone mass, from purging for eleven years to the abuse I have done to my body.

I also want to share what I have learned about the gurus of dieting. They are scattered across all of our lives, we the desperate, and not only in our own country and century but throughout history. I wanted to know something about these diet gurus, who they are and why they chose to try to lead the way to health in their times and in their own lives.

And I want to tell my own story in all its gory details, so that others might see that they do not have to stay on the same path I was on. We all are looking for solutions; I want to share the story of how I came to slay (many of) the demons and conquer the food.

CHAPTER 1

MY JOURNEY

The First Decade—Running

We ourselves are the battleground . . . All the power of
transcendence is within us. Tap into it and you tap into
the divine itself.

—DENG MING-DAO

I was born in Seattle, Washington, on May 1, 1939. That
year, Germany invaded Poland. The Daughters of the
American Revolution refused to let Marian Anderson
sing at Constitution Hall in Washington, D.C., so Eleanor Roosevelt resigned from the DAR in protest and
facilitated Anderson's concert at the Lincoln Memorial. Marjorie Kinnan Rawlings's *The Yearling* won the
Pulitzer Prize. Maxwell Perkins, who also edited Ernest
Hemingway and F. Scott Fitzgerald, had given her good
advice: He told her to write about her own life.

My father would read *The Yearling* to me from his copy

in Braille, pausing as he read to tell me, first, that a woman could win the Pulitzer, and, second, that a woman could do anything she set her mind to. He said I should always tell my own story, as she had told hers. Daddy was telling his, on his radio show, to his children, and in his journals.

Unfortunately, Mother burned Daddy's journals after his death.

But I always knew what he meant.

Daddy and Mommy and I lived in a little house on a hill with a lawn that sloped down to the street, and there are pictures of me after a rare snowstorm going down that hill on a sled. And there I am again, in my pigtails in the summer sun, my naked body splashing in the wash-tub, a huge smile on my face. Even the black-and-white pictures show that I was blond, with curls and a bright pair of eyes.

As a tiny girl, I knew that my father was blind. I tried to make him see me; I talked and danced and sang. I knew he was fighting some kind of battle. But not because he could not see—he seemed to be perfectly at ease with that, even as he felt my face to know what I looked like. He would sometimes say there were advantages to being blind, like being able to read in the dark. No, it was some other battle.

I remember running, being excited, moving fast, al-most in a blur. I was in a hurry from the start, walking at nine months, trying to catch up before I ever had a clue where I was headed. I knew I had to keep up with my blind, brilliant, talented father and with my mother who was as thin as a whip and always cooking, cleaning, driving my dad to the radio station to do his show, making my bed, braiding my hair, making my clothes on her Singer sewing machine. The Singer caught my imagination and I would hum along with the treadle. It was hurry, hurry, hurry, there was so much to be done, so much to see—I was seeing for my dad and soon I was the eldest of five siblings and running around helping my mother take care of them, changing diapers, cooking, babysitting. I would take a break and then it was back on the track, hurrying to get to somewhere.

The only time I really stopped hurrying was when I was singing, playing the piano, reading, or acting in a play. As a child, I was trained in the skills that would be required for me to survive, and to thrive. To shine on the stage, entertaining. What was missing in my training was the "rule book"—how to survive, how to get through life when I was not doing that thing that is my passion, when I was not onstage. Finding out how to live out of the spotlight (and in the spotlight, finally) was something I would have to nearly die to learn.

There are pictures of my grandparents at their golden wedding anniversary in 1943 on their porch in Seattle and the wedding cake that I devoured when no one was looking, making a dent in the back of the pristine white layers—a dent I covered over with more frosting. I did not want to be scolded on their special day, sent to my room or made an example of: Look at her, ruining that nice wedding cake.

My father, who had been blind from the age of four, was a man who saw more than most men I have known—sensitive, gifted, and inspiring in the way he managed every day of his sightlessness. Photographs of my father and the family crop up in boxes, in letters, in the folders my mother saved, folders of report cards and prom notices and newspaper articles about my father, and me, and the family. Photos of Daddy's fraternity brother Holden Bowler, who was my godfather and who had a golden voice like my dad. They had been in Phi Gamma Delta at the University of Idaho.

Daddy was an alcoholic, born with the genetic disposition to the illness, a Jekyll and Hyde who could turn from charming to terrifying when he was at his worst. He drank whiskey—Johnnie Walker and Four Roses— and like me, he loved sugar and kept chocolate-covered cherries in his sock drawer where he hid what he thought was his secret. All of us children knew they were there, whispering to us from among his tidy, carefully folded socks. We would haunt his sock drawer and his other sugar hiding spots. Over time, I would find them all.

He would dig into sweets, pies, cakes, divinity, fudge with the exuberance of an addict and the joy of a satisfied husband. Mother, who did not seem to have our compulsions, was a fabulous baker and cook—as well as chauffeur, friend, and fan of my father's many talents, even when he was too drunk to notice.

My father had a head of beautiful, full, mostly auburn hair tinged only slightly gray, right up to the time he died at fifty-seven. He was always working on keeping his weight down. He would mow the lawn barefooted so he could "see" where he was going, getting the feel of the grass under his toes. He sometimes smoked—referring to his cigarettes as "coffin nails"—lecturing all the while about the dangers of smoking. His pipe was always in the pocket of whatever jacket he was wearing, and he packed the bowl with Old Briar cherry-flavored tobacco, though he occasionally smoked a cigar. I thought that a pipe tasted better than any cigarette I ever smoked.

Daddy was also a reader, and in our house, books were required possessions. My father read to all of us children from the time we were tiny. He would sit on the edge of my bed and run his fingers over the pages of the big Braille volumes from the Library of Congress—history, mystery, and the Russians—*War and Peace*, *The Double*, Chekhov. The books he read were big, weighty tomes that stood many feet high stacked against the wall. He once told me that when he could not sleep he would count the books he had read in his lifetime—hundreds of books, in Braille or on what he referred to as "talking books." They arrived bound in heavy twine-wound squares. Daddy thought if you had not read *Moby-Dick* by the time you were seven, there must be something wrong with you.

Reading has been a lifelong obsession of mine, a pre-occupation. As I read I began to learn what others did to control their demons. There were spiritual routes, and there were pragmatic ones as well. The two, for me, are inextricably linked. I always had a belief in some higher power in the world. I went to church, sang in the choir, loved the hymns. I learned to pray early in my life, wishing our Methodist practices could magically invoke the smoke and mirrors and meditations of the Catholic Church. Bring on Thomas Merton, bring on the saints! I longed for drama!

I discovered that there have always been pilgrims in the search for abstinence from food, alcohol, and drugs, as well as relief from despair and depression. There were those who were looking, as I was, for a spiritually uplifted life. And as I got older I began to pray for a different relationship with food and alcohol.

I knew early on that we were a family troubled by alcoholism and some kind of addiction to food. There were arguments about the liquor cabinet—Mother would lock it up and Daddy would break the lock in the middle of the night.

And I have come to understand that the effects of addiction are not limited to the drinker or the eater but have an impact on the entire family, and sometimes on our friends, too. The denial, the recovery, the relapses—

they affect everyone. And I would come to understand that food addiction, like alcoholism, does not play favorites. But at that time I was sure our family had been singled out because of some moral defect of which we had no memory or knowledge. I slowly began to understand that these illnesses strike the rich and the poor, men and women, the infamous and the famous, peasants and royalty, housewives and bankers.

I followed in my father's footsteps, beginning with music and the piano lessons and soon with the passion for alcohol and sugar. I was transfixed by the desserts my mother whipped up, whirling her right arm in a circle until the confection was fluffy. She added crushed pecans to the mix, and I got to lick the spoon and the bowl. From the age of three I knew that nothing could make me happier than devouring sugar in any form, at any time. Best were the fudge and divinity, the pies with meringue or made of apples or pumpkin, the Toll House cookies. Sugar fueled my race through life.

It was the beginning of my dance with the devil.

CHAPTER 2

LIVES OF THE DIET GURUS

Lord Byron

> She walks in beauty, like the night
> Of cloudless climes and starry skies . . .
>
> —LORD BYRON, "SHE WALKS IN BEAUTY"

Lord Byron, the English poet born in London on January 22, 1788, knew all about dieting to control his rampant problems with food. The first celebrity dieter had entered the world. From his reputation and the observations of others, he was said to be anorexic as well as bulimic. He was brilliant and world famous at an early age, a part of the Romantic movement, and probably the first pop idol to recommend diets to his fans and friends.

His mother was Catherine Gordon and his father was Captain John "Mad Jack" Byron, who ran off to France with his mistress when Byron was a baby. Byron was raised in impoverished circumstances, by a mother he resented, blaming her for the clubfoot with which he was born.

When he was ten, Byron was thrust from poverty to nobility when he inherited the English title of 6th Baron Byron of Rochdale on the death of his uncle Lord Byron, known as the "Wicked Lord." The "Wicked" appellation came as a result of a duel in 1765 in which Baron Byron killed his cousin Baron William Chaworth following an argument about who had more game on his estate. The murder was ruled manslaughter and Baron Byron was given a light fine. He seems to have worn the "Wicked" with pride, but began to fall into madness after the scandal, shooting one of his coachmen to death and depleting his fortune and holdings so that a son he despised would not inherit anything. When Byron the Wicked died, his only nephew inherited his uncle's "legacy of misery," since all other heirs were deceased.

Lord Byron and his mother moved to Newstead Abbey, the Byron family estate in Nottinghamshire. Byron was sent to Harrow, a boarding school where he quickly attained the reputation of being a troubled young man. Yet when he got to Trinity College, Cambridge, Byron was popular on campus, drinking and gambling with zeal. He had earlier fallen in love with his cousin, Mary Chaworth, but while he was at Trinity, she had married another man.

Fugitive Pieces, Byron's premier poetry adventure, was published anonymously in 1806. His dance with the demon of weight obsessions and food compulsion had already begun. Since it was almost unheard of to have your own personal scale, Berry Brothers and Rudd, a London wine-and-cheese shop, allowed stylish men-about-town to weigh themselves on the industrial scales that were suspended by metal chains from the ceiling in the basement of the shop. We can imagine the dank aromas of sides of beef and wheels of Edam and Swiss cheese that were hauled on and off the metal surface on which these young men would lie, probably after disrobing as fully as possible. It must have been an assault to the senses but apparently worth it.

From carefully kept records at Berry Brothers we learn that in 1806, Byron weighed 182 pounds. By 1811 he was down to 126 pounds, a loss of nearly 70 pounds. Beau Brummell, the "English Dandy," made forty visits to Berry Brothers to weigh himself. Usually in deep debt, Brummell was a fashion icon who abandoned the upper-class dress of the English and created the shirt-and-tie model that continues to the present time. Over the course of his trips to Berry Brothers, Brummel's weight went from 168 down to 140.

At Cambridge Lord Byron wore heavy wool sweaters in order to sweat (and probably to hide his girth) and his fans followed suit, wearing heavy woolen sweaters and copying his diet of vinegar, rice, and potatoes; his habit of smoking cigars to curb his appetite; and his practice of eating "scantily" and then gorging on huge meals.

Byron also started the fashion of taking huge doses of magnesia—the primary ingredient of many laxatives—to control his weight.

At twenty, Byron began his love affair with Greece during his Grand Tour after graduating from university. In a letter to his half sister, Augusta Leigh, he wrote: "If I am a poet . . . the air of Greece has made me one."

Upon his return to the British Isles, his long poem *Childe Harold's Pilgrimage* was published. The poem was about a lost soul wandering through the world and ostensibly about Byron's journeys through Portugal, Greece, and the Aegean, and the first printing sold out in three days. "I awoke one morning and found myself famous," he would say.

Amid writing poetry and fighting in wars, he was also dieting and publicly declaiming to all who would listen his culinary discoveries, which must have been spread by word of mouth, if you will forgive the pun, as I can find no evidence that Byron published anything about his diets, only that they were passed on by those who knew him to those who followed him. It is said that he would purge after eating large meals. He was famous for the "potatoes and vinegar diet," which he used and recommended to others for weight loss or weight maintenance. He was known as being "mad, bad and dangerous," as madness was considered in those times to be the cause of homosexuality.

Byron's love affairs—with Mary Chaworth, John

Edleston, Mary Duff, Claire Clairmont, and, it is thought, Augusta Leigh, his half sister—were often violent. His moods swung wildly; his future biographers would claim that he suffered from bipolar disorder. Byron's clubfoot may have prompted the violent exercise in which he indulged to keep fit. He insisted on riding, boxing, and swimming in a vigorously obsessive manner to keep his weight down. He also engaged in "exercise bulimia," the current name for the effort to get the pounds off that the food puts on. A vicious cycle at best, as I know too well. Louise Foxcroft, in *Corsets and Calories*, her compendium of the proponents of dieting, reports that Dr. George Beard, a well-known physician in London, was quoted as saying, "Impressionable romantics are restricting themselves to vinegar and rice to get the fashionably thin and pale look. Our young ladies live all their growing girlhood in semi-starvation, incurring the horror of the disciplines of Lord Byron."

Byron's habits—eating very little, then devouring huge meals, then drinking large amounts of magnesium to purge—worried people who were not among his growing audience of followers. Byron himself often suggested, "A woman should never be seen eating or drinking, unless it be lobster salad and champagne, the only truly feminine and becoming viands."

In 1815, Byron married Annabella Milbanke, whom he introduced at once to Augusta. On their first visit to Augusta's home, while her husband was away, Annabella slept alone in one bedroom while Byron was locked in what must have been a passionate meeting with his half sister in another. He and Annabella had a daughter, Augusta Ada, and after a year of a marriage that was described as miserable, Annabella left him, publicly accusing her former husband of incest and abuse. England then took up the cry against Byron's amoral behavior. His great poems kept coming, but Byron left England for good, his reputation in tatters, his finances a disaster. But nothing seemed to stop his outpouring of beautiful poetry. *The Siege of Corinth* and *Parisina,* two of his greatest poems, were published during this time.

In May 1816 Byron arrived in Lake Geneva, a new hot spot for wealthy tourists and bohemians. He had been invited by Claire Clairmont, with whom he was having an affair, to Villa Diodati, the most fashionable resort on the lake. Byron arrived in an elegant coach with half a dozen footmen. His personal physician, John Polidori, who had a yearning to write poetry, accompanied him. The rest of Byron's party included a peacock, a monkey, and a dog.

Byron settled in with the beautiful and very young Claire at the villa, where he met up with Percy Bysshe Shelley, who was also newly famous. Shelley was in favor of free love and did not believe in God. Atheism was coming into fashion, led by many artists and poets, and Shelley, now twenty-three, spoke and wrote eloquently on atheism.

Claire, who was eighteen, was the sister of Mary Wollstonecraft Godwin (who would marry Shelley later that year). Byron and Shelley quickly became friends. Shelley, Mary, and Claire, as well as Polidori, began their holiday at the castle on the lake.

Over a rainy weekend, the five friends read *Fantasmagoriana,* a French anthology of ghost stories. After finishing the book, they agreed to go to their rooms and try writing their own short horror stories. It was out of this reading binge that Byron wrote "Fragment of a Novel"—later included as a postscript to *Mazeppa,* the story of a Cossack who is tied naked to a wild horse— one of the earliest stories of vampires written in English. For his assignment, Polidori wrote "The Vampyre," and Mary Shelley wrote *Frankenstein.* A fine feast of phantasmagoria, certainly, and a great result of a gathering of friends bent on creativity.

By now, it is said that Byron was living on slices of toast and tea, dinners of vegetables and green tea. He was ruining his health and was heard to say that dieting was leading to "more than half our maladies." He chainsmoked cigars to suppress his appetite. His fans and followers not only read his poetry but followed his advice on diets and also, like their hero, smoked as many cigarettes and cigars as possible.

The Greeks revered Byron as a national hero since he had supported them in their War of Independence from Ottoman rule, serving in the Greek army against the Turks in 1821. At the time of his death, Byron was again fighting against the Ottoman Empire in the Greek and English armies. On April 19, 1824, the day before his troops were to attack the Turks at Corinth, Byron died from an infection and fever. He was embalmed and it is said that his heart was cut out by the Greeks and buried in Missolonghi, near the site of his last intended battle. Today the Greeks still pay homage to Byron's heart, as well as his spirit. His heartless body was sent to England to be entombed at Westminster Abbey, but it was decided by the church that Byron's "questionable morality" would prevent his remains from being buried in the church. In the England of the nineteenth century, the government could and did hang people who were overtly homosexual, and therefore Byron's body lay in state for two days in London as huge crowds lined up to pay their respects. After a procession that was half a mile long, Byron was finally interred at the Church of St. Mary Magdalene in Northamptonshire. Augusta Ada was eventually buried alongside him in the same remote crypt. Boatswain, his faithful dog, has a fine memorial near his master's grave, but there is no memorial for Byron himself. It took 124 years before Byron's plaque was installed at Westminster Abbey in 1969, in the Poets' Corner, alongside those of Chaucer, Spenser, and Shakespeare, where he truly belongs.

It is said that had Byron succeeded in his support of Greece against the Turks, he might have been named

King of Greece. Byron's love affairs were mostly a disaster, as were most of his experiments with diet, but his journey with food is remarkable for its example of how far one can go to keep thin. The poet's food obsession and nightmare demons pursued him in spite of the brilliance of his poetry. Some believe that creative people have a hound with hungry jaws chasing them down the corridors of beauty. When slaying demons we must be careful not to slay the one that might be responsible for the great things we do in our lives.

Hard to tell, often, which is which.

As well as being a magnificent poet and a dashingly charismatic lover, Byron was a king of eating-disorder literature. He was honest and brave, fighting a war not only in Greece and with his sexual obsessions but in his own body. It was a war that he, like many of us, could not win.

CHAPTER 3

MY JOURNEY

The Forties

My weaknesses have always been food and men—in that order.

—DOLLY PARTON

My mother always prepared simple meals. We had chicken on Sundays, and roast turkeys were the high point of the holiday dinners. *The Joy of Cooking* was on her kitchen counter, with its pages sporting the occasional turned-down corner and gravy stains, a well-loved and well-used book. She was also a whiz at the desserts. Her divinity and chocolate fudge were dream inducing, and they were always there, the homemade pies and cookies in abundance, rum-soaked fruitcakes for the holidays, and sugar cookies that we decorated with colored frostings and pearl sparkles. It was heavenly, and even as a child I appreciated the love she put into cooking for us.

But the sugar and the trimmings were even then digging their claws into my flesh.

When I was four, we moved to Los Angeles. My dad
got a great new job in Hollywood at CBS, on a daily
radio show. He sometimes commuted by bus and sometimes was driven by Mother in Claudia, our black Buick.
Soon after my fifth birthday, my parents sent me to my
first piano lessons.

In those years—those long-lost days—it was all right
to send a six- or seven-year-old on the bus from West Los
Angeles to Santa Monica. On the way to music lessons,
my piano scores tucked under my arm, I would soothe
the savage beast with Bazooka Bubble Gum, Necco
Wafers, Almond Joys, Mud Pies, and Peppermint Patties.
I spent the change from the bus fare on sugar, and would
have loved to have marshmallows in my sandwiches like
some kids, but which I never got because my mother was
a pure peanut-butter-and-jelly kind of mom, on whole
grain! There might be a twist of waxed paper filled with
raisins in my lunch bag and usually an apple, and the most
extreme gesture my mother would make toward my love
of sugar was the dime she pressed into my hand as I left
for school, ten cents for a chocolate milk. I would have
been happy to eat Candy Corn all year, cotton candy
every afternoon, and a bag of Hershey Kisses every night.
We didn't usually have this type of food in the house,
and as a result I can remember often bingeing on raw
oatmeal (nutritionists would say that was a better choice

than a Mars bar) but I was bingeing nonetheless, and if I could have had sugar I would have had it while reading *The Count of Monte Cristo*. The pattern was set, and reading was very often part of it. It got so that I could, and still can, read *The Count of Monte Cristo* while practicing scales and doing Hanon exercises on the piano! (Nowadays it might be *The Girl with the Dragon Tattoo*.) For someone who was destined to have a public life, I had a distinct passion for hiding and bingeing.

My father, in his long musical career, was often asked to perform at fund-raisers. On one such night in 1948, my mom was busy so I asked to go with my dad to a fund-raiser for the Salk vaccine. Mom said yes, and when we got there, someone thought it would be a cute idea to put me, age eight at the time, into the iron lung to illustrate how it worked!

I was lifted up and into the oval-shaped machine and laid down on a white sheet. Someone shut the glass lid above my body and turned on the chuffing, puffing machine, which proceeded to make my chest move up and down with no effort on my part. I remember that after being terrified when the lid closed and the noise started, I was soon delighted with the experience.

My mother, when she found out, was appalled.

"Charles," she said to my dad, "how could you let them do that to her!" Later, when I had polio, she would blame it on the iron lung. "That goddamned iron lung!" she would say.

There would be concerts, appearances on my father's radio show, in the school shows, in piano recitals. I began to feel the pressure mounting. As I grew up, turning nine and ten, sugar in all its many forms became a drug for me. It soothed my anxiety and sense of doom. I think the expectations of my parents and teachers were part of the spiral of emotions. I knew, and my family knew, that I was going to be a professional musician someday like my father. They seemed to agree it could be a long and very winding road and there might be roadblocks but that I would manage. Or they assumed I would, and I took their faith in me to heart.

What I did not know was that most of my obstacles would involve food and alcohol.

CHAPTER 4

LIVES OF THE DIET GURUS

Gayelord Hauser—The Man Who Invented

the Celebrity Diet

When we lived in West Los Angeles, my father made a lot of friends during his stint on CBS. I remember many days Mom would drive him to work from our home at 11572 Mississippi Avenue, up Santa Monica Boulevard, past trees in the parks of Beverly Hills, trees I still see to this day on my trips to La-La Land. The mountains were as clear as day then, the air clean, the light beautiful, and once in a while, after a rain, you could still see the hills above Laurel Canyon reaching down to Sunset Strip and tucking in the houses where Joni Mitchell and David Crosby and Stephen Stills would later write songs and dream of fame. Hollywood today is like Hollywood in 1945, full of talented people living in what they think of as Nirvana.

Many of Daddy's new friends were clients of Gayelord Hauser, the "Nutritionist to the Stars." Daddy took to Hauser's methods with a vengeance and there was no white bread in our house, no white rice, no junk. He used Hauser's suggested hangover cure of blackstrap molasses, wheat germ, yogurt, vitamin D, and raw eggs mixed in a blender. For years we had a regular health spa in our kitchen—first in West Los Angeles and then in Denver. Hauser and his ideas about nutrition permeated our home and helped my father think he could deal with his addictions to alcohol and food.

Hauser had been born Helmut Eugene Benjamin Gellert in Tübingen, Germany, in 1895 and spent the first years of his life there with his brother, Otto, his mother, Agate, and his father, Christian, who was a teacher. In August 1911, the sixteen-year-old Hauser sailed to America in steerage on the SS *George Washington* and passed through immigration on Ellis Island. From New York, he traveled to Chicago to join Otto, who had immigrated and become a citizen, and was now a pastor.

In his late teens, Hauser developed tuberculosis of the hip, a chronic bacterial infection that without proper treatment eventually destroys the hip and can be fatal. This rare TB occurs in about 15 percent of tubercular cases. Today, treatment for this illness would consist of physical and drug therapy, usually antibiotics. But there were no antibiotics in 1913, when Hauser was infected.

At the hospital where Hauser was diagnosed, his doctors told him to prepare to die. He refused to give up hope and began a search to find someone who could help him regain his health. His treatment included many operations that proved unsuccessful in stopping the spread of the disease. His doctors declared him hopeless.

Desperate to save his life, Hauser began to hunt for alternatives. He was led to Dr. Benedict Lust, a German immigrant who founded the American School of Naturopathy. Lust was one of the first to introduce the practice of alternative medicine and diet in the United States. His approach encouraged natural cures, increased fiber intake, and reduced saturated fats. When Hauser's condition began to improve after following Lust's prescriptions, he was jubilant. Lust then suggested that Hauser go to Switzerland, where there were doctors who were practicing the new "food science," which was having positive effects on other illnesses that did not respond to Western medicine. There among the Alps, Hauser met Brother Maier, a monk, who put him on a diet of fruit juice, vegetarian broth, and herbs.

Soon Hauser's tubercular hip went into complete remission, never to return. His interest in the power of diet over illness drew him to study nutrition in Vienna, Zurich, Copenhagen, and Dresden, where the ancient practice of naturopathic medicine was flowering. Hauser became aware of homeopathic medicine, a method discovered by Samuel Hahnemann, who had studied the power of "like curing like" while investigating the uses of quinine in healing malaria. In 1796, Hahnemann had published his finding that a tiny speck of something that was dangerous in larger doses could cure many diseases. It was revolutionary and is still used in many countries.

When he returned to the United States, Hauser received degrees in naturopathy and chiropractics from a number of institutions. He changed his name to Gaylord Hauser and began touring the Midwest, speaking about the five "wonder foods": yogurt, brewer's yeast, powdered milk, wheat germ, and blackstrap molasses, which he recommended for overall physical health. He proclaimed sugar to be poison and went into business with his brother-in-law Sebastian Gysin to merchandise Swiss Kriss, a natural laxative product for cleansing the digestive tract that was invented by Gysin's company, Modern Products. He also created broths and seasonings that can be found in many health food stores to this day under the Modern Products label.

Hauser also urged people to avoid eating starch (white bread, pasta, potatoes, gluten) and red meat, and after he moved to Hollywood in 1927, he attracted more famous clients. Grace Kelly, Jeanne Moreau, and Ingrid Bergman sought his help with their health issues.

Hauser was said to be "nattily good-looking, brash and exuberant." His understanding of cucumber masks for the face (to ward off the after-effects of alcohol), and of what made skin shine, eyes brighten, bodies slim, illness flee, and health return, helped to attract Queen Alexandra of Yugoslavia, Baron Rothschild, Mae West,

Adele Astaire, Marlene Dietrich, the Duchess of Windsor, Paulette Goddard, Gloria Swanson, and Greta Garbo. Even Elizabeth Arden (the founder of the line of beauty products, one of which, the Eight Hour Cream, was designed for her horses) was one of Hauser's clients. She was especially fond of the slant board, another of Hauser's ideas, on which you lie, head down and feet elevated, to improve circulation and for relaxation.

In Hollywood, Hauser's clients were people my father had begun to meet at parties and drink with after hours. Mercedes McCambridge (an actor with two stars on Hollywood's Walk of Fame), Red Skelton, and Bob Hope, and the various voices of the Shadow—James La Curto, Frank Readick Jr., Orson Welles—these were some of the people Daddy interviewed on his radio show and with whom he shared ideas. In the smoky, star-crowded bars near the CBS studios, my dark-haired, good-looking, man-about-town dad was sometimes mistaken for Mickey Rooney. These moments of mistaken identity or just too much to drink with a pal at the bars often made him late for dinner and occasionally turned my mother into a different person while she awaited his arrival late at night. Along with his actor friends, Daddy also soon discovered Hauser's tiger's milk and raw eggs hangover cure, brown rice, and multigrain bread. Wonder foods.

After Daddy started doing things the Hauser way, there would be lectures on nutrition, shouted among the loud discourse on politics and report cards at our dinner table along with rants on the dangers of cigarettes. By then I was sneaking trips to neighborhood stores during my bus rides to piano lessons and walks to school to get the forbidden sugar of my own passions. But I wasn't smoking yet! That would come later, in spite of my father's lectures about coffin nails.

One of Hauser's little instructions to his clients who wanted to get rid of the "jelly belly" that sometimes comes with losing weight was to practice "crunching the belly muscles" a few times a day. This advice he gave out freely, and people said they liked it because you didn't need expensive shoes or special outfits from the May Company or JCPenney! He also pointed out that, as all the modern-day exercise instructors know, regular crunches, no matter how many you might fit into an hour-long exercise session, aren't enough.

No wonder the stars loved him, in more ways than one!

Hauser had a long friendship with Garbo, about which much has been written. In the early forties, she introduced him to her friend Frey Brown, a promising young actor who soon became Hauser's lover. Hauser bought a villa in Taormina, Italy, in 1950, and he and Brown began to spend many months of the year there. Garbo was known to visit them on the island, disguising herself with scarves and hats, but still often recognized by Hauser's neighbors and the press.

Hauser and Brown lived together until Brown's death in 1979.

Hauser wrote many books, beginning in 1930 with *Harmonized Food Selection: Including the Famous Hauser Body Building System*. Perhaps the most famous of his writings was *Look Younger, Live Longer,* which was serialized in *Reader's Digest* in English as well as in Braille, which is how my father found it.

Hauser has been immortalized in the diet-conscious history of our lives and was the first commercially successful American "nutritionist" to tell the beautiful people how they could stay younger-looking, fit, and healthy. Western doctors didn't like Hauser, who claimed that many of the illnesses they treated were better handled with improved diet, one that excluded white bread, white flour, sugar, wheat, starch, and most grains. He recommended yogurt, hard to find in the thirties and forties, and many kinds of vitamins and minerals that were also difficult to lay your hands on then. Now you can buy wheat- and gluten-free food, sort through the delicious choices of fresh vegetables, and find every kind of yogurt imaginable.

Hauser lived a happy and healthy life until his death in 1984 at eighty-nine. In pop culture, in song, and in health-food stores, in our pursuit of healthy bodies free of sugar and junk, enlivened with yogurt and cucumber masks and products like Swiss Kriss, in tummy crunches and brewer's yeast, blackstrap molasses and raw eggs for a hangover, Hauser's fame lives on. Even in the Broadway production *New Faces of 1952*, Eartha Kitt helped raise Hauser's profile in the cultural top ten when she sang:

Chiang Kai-shek sends me pots of tea,
Gayelord Hauser sends me Vitamin D . . .
And, furthermore, Ike likes me.

CHAPTER 5

MY JOURNEY

Into the Fifties—Music, Music, Music, and My Galloping Food Addiction

The goal of life is to make your heartbeat match the beat
of the universe, to match your nature with Nature.

—JOSEPH CAMPBELL

In 1949 my father lost his great job in Hollywood at CBS,
but he got a better job, and we moved to Denver and the
Rocky Mountains. In the fifties in Denver, our lives were
full of the fame brought to us by my father's popularity
on the radio. He became a staple in the lives of Denver's
residents with his daily radio program that started his lis-
teners' days with his enthusiasm, readings of poetry, Mae
West jokes, and his beautiful singing voice.

I was nine when we moved. We reveled in the beauty
of the mountains. My parents at once fell in love with
the city and the state and we would take trips up into the
mountains, often on the weekend, with a picnic lunch

of fried chicken and potato salad (with sweet gherkins), celery and carrot sticks, and a dip made from dried onion soup mix and sour cream; there would be sugar-filled homemade brownies, a jug of Kool-Aid and ice, and beer for Daddy. We would find a spot on the Boulder Canyon road or the Peak to Peak Highway, where, in those years, you could pull to the side of the road and hike half a mile to a waterfall, where we would put down our blanket, shell out our forks and knives and napkins, grab colored aluminum "glasses" (the kind you won from gas stations—beautiful colors, blue and bronze, silver and green, shiny pink and purple). Our picnic would last all afternoon, and between courses we would hike a ways up the mountain, finding a spot where we could see Denver or Boulder. When the air cooled and the sun started down between the canyon walls, we would pack up our things and hike back to the car.

Then mother would drive us to Denver, with Daddy backseat driving, and we would settle down in front of the television set for the Sunday TV shows—*Omnibus, The Jack Benny Program,* and *What's My Line?* Our faces would be burned and our tummies full. For supper there would be leftover chicken and brownies, double and triple helpings for me, and early to bed with our exhausted bodies bathed and dried and our feet powdered. Thankfully Daddy would be sober, the Sunday beer safely digested, his heart full of the sound and fury of the waterfall and the thoughts of his children sleeping.

Growing up, I felt the pressures of living in a big family and having many responsibilities. As the eldest of five siblings, there were always chores: babysitting, cooking, cleaning, washing and ironing clothes, even learning to sew on the Singer sewing machine that lived in my mother's bedroom. I was constantly helping Mom turn out clothes for me and Holly, my sister, and three brothers, Denver John, David, and Michael. I know I was terrified a lot of the time, but about what? I don't know. I only know I was watching my father's struggle with alcohol and noticing there was a shadow that was slowly creeping into our lives.

There were, of course, happy times! Now in their late thirties, Daddy and my godfather, Holden Bowler, were still carrying on like college kids, in their summer shorts, chasing each other through our backyard, one of them with a garden hose going full blast, spraying water. One who could see, and one who could not. There are pictures of me running beside my father and my godfather, splashing through the water—you can almost hear my screams of delight.

But there were nights when my father would weep bitterly after a day of drinking, and I felt that having an alcoholic in the family was shameful. As I shivered in my bed and heard his sobs, unable to help him, to comfort him, I felt that his drinking was in some way my fault. Maybe I was absorbing my father's pain.

When I was ten, I began to feel an ache in my right

hip. I told the nurse at school about it, and she said it must be growing pains, which would pass. They did not pass and one day a doctor came to visit me at home. He brought a little hammer with a rubber head on it and tap-tap-tapped my right knee, which hurt like hell. By that evening I had been admitted to Children's Hospital Colorado on Nineteenth Street. The doctor told my parents I had polio.

Poliomyelitis, as it was known before the vaccine was approved, had caused paralysis and death for centuries, although until the fifties there were few true epidemics. Now fear of polio was terrifying populations all across the United States—the government was closing schools and pools, the disease was threatening young and old, paralyzing or killing half a million people a year at its peak.

I spent April and May of 1950 at Children's Hospital. The first month was in total isolation in a little room with a window looking out onto the parkway, where I could hear the birds singing and watch as the spring spread its brilliance across the treetops and among the grasses and purple and blue buds in the gardens and up toward the Rocky Mountain peaks. It was a month that passed slowly—a month of no visitors, not even my parents. Everything—including my books, my clothes, even the flowers that friends and family sent, even the tins of brownies and divinity that my mother made for me—was put through a sterilizing machine that turned them black. My father wrote me letters—also sterilized and black around the edges—in which he was encouraging, reminding me that Franklin Roosevelt had been totally paralyzed below the waist by polio. In spite of his crippled legs, the thirty-second president of the United States never let his condition stop him. My father was graphic in his description of Roosevelt's struggles, talking about the long recovery at Warm Springs, Georgia, all the rehab he had to have, his desire to appear able to walk, the hiding of the crutches, all more information than my circumstances might have called for. I don't remember whether his letters terrified me or gave me comfort. But Daddy thought it would help me to know that the father of the New Deal had been paralyzed by the illness from which I was suffering. Maybe he was right.

I spent the days reading (*White Fang* and *Moby-Dick*) and making a glass of juice—usually pineapple—last half the morning. The juice was brought on carts and handed through the sterilizer by the civilian volunteers—ladies in blue dresses and little blue hats and big smiles. I would dip my finger in the glass and suck off the sweet juice; I could never get enough to eat. Even in pain, with a fever, and with medication being poured down my throat all day, I had to be putting things to eat and drink in my mouth, particularly when I was reading.

The second month of my incarceration (I thought of it as jail), I was making little slippers out of colored plastic and longing for my mother's cooking (in 1950 the food in hospitals was not so great, unappealing even to me). But I was enjoying being able to read from morning till night, and soon the goodies were now making it to my room without having to be put through the sterilizer!

At first the paralysis was in my right hip, but I was lucky not to have been left with a limp after my months in the hospital and recovering. I was held back a year in school, but that made up for having been jumped ahead a year when we moved to Denver. I came out of the hospital to bundles of spring flowers, the purples and whites, violets and baby rosebuds. There is a picture of me hugging those flowers and the stuffed lamb my mother gave me. I recovered quickly and returned to total health, which I did not question. I had such faith in my health. The most wonderful thing was I was allowed to have all the sugar I wanted.

It was upon my return from the hospital that my father found a new piano teacher for me: Dr. Antonia Brico. She was strict but warm, old-fashioned in her demeanor (one would say European), a complete classical miracle in all her history and training, and she was famous in Denver. I would soon discover that she was world-famous and her amazing life would be revealed to me in many hours poring over her press releases as I helped her glue them into huge black scrapbooks. I would come to love her, but that first day I was terrified on meeting her— she was very imposing, with a large nose and a fierce gaze that focused on my plaid dress, my oxford shoes, and my shaking fingers. I played on her great Steinway (one of two in her studio that was filled with portraits of Beethoven and Bach who stared down at me from the walls), and after I put my hands back onto my lap, she was very quiet for a while, looking at me and then at my parents. She cleared her throat and said she would take me as a student, even though my technique was terrible and she would have her work cut out for her. Lucky me, I would also have my work cut out for me, and for the next six years I studied with Brico, the strict, Dutch Italian perfectionist.

Music—playing the piano, singing on my father's shows, performing in school shows, and even having the lead in *Snow White and the Seven Dwarfs* and singing "Some Day My Prince Will Come"—probably saved my sanity to some degree growing up. I studied a Mozart concerto to play with Brico's orchestra. (Brico, who had been a famous conductor in New York and Europe, and even had her own orchestra in New York during World War II, had formed an orchestra in Denver, the Denver Businessmen's Orchestra, when she had been denied the podium of the Denver Symphony.) I sang in school and church choirs, in *South Pacific,* and in Brico's opera choruses, all the while living in an increasingly chaotic home as my father's alcoholism progressed. I am sure the drinking in my home started my journey to the dark thoughts and depression that would haunt me for years.

But when I was growing up, people did not talk about

these things. We, like many families, had no idea what was wrong with us. Gayelord Hauser was about as close as we ever got to the real solution, and meanwhile, Daddy's alcoholism and what we would now call my mother's untreated codependency were wearing away the fabric of our family. No one in our family and not one of the doctors who treated us ever talked about Daddy's drinking (that I know of) until later in his life when I sent him to see a psychiatrist who said she would not treat him because he refused to talk about his drinking. I was certainly not able to speak of these things to teachers, or to my mother or father. I eventually was ashamed to invite people to our home, which had been full of laughter, friends, and family in earlier years. The ravages of drinking were evident, from the rages of my dad in his cups to my mother's silent scorn and tears at my father's womanizing (of which I was aware, since it was not exactly hidden, and also because he shared with me certain details of his wandering).

I certainly had the gene pool for addiction. I always thought I needed something to avert the disaster I felt moving in on me from every side, not knowing that food and alcohol were already playing a large part in my feelings of devastation.

When I was eleven, Brico told me (she never asked) that I was going to play a Mozart piano concerto with her orchestra: K. 365, written by Mozart for himself and his sister, Nannerl, when they were both very young children. I would be playing with Danno Guerrero, who was three years older than I.

And so I began studying and practicing, sitting at our Baldwin grand for two hours every day after school, playing Czerny and Chopin, Debussy and Beethoven. Every few months we would have a rehearsal, Danny and I. Practice was always part of my life, an imposed discipline. Danny (now a well-known musician on the West Coast) and I gave what was called a sparkling performance with the symphony while the blizzard that descended on Colorado on February 21 folded the city in crystal white with snowdrifts that were ten feet in places. It did not mar our enthusiasm or our brave audience's response. I was dressed in a white organdy off-the-shoulder dress, very much a Doris Day creation, and my heart soared at the sense of accomplishment that came when I stepped into the spotlights at the end of the evening and took my bows.

A year later, the glow was off of my life, I suppose. It had eroded a bit since my triumph with the Mozart. I was still working very hard at the piano and practicing a piece by Liszt called "La Campanella," a wrenching business of about a thousand notes per minute, it seemed to me—brilliant-sounding when you got it right, as though all the bells of every cathedral in the country were going off at once, but when you didn't, it sounded at best like a traffic jam. It was a demanding piece I was not very fond of, but Brico had assigned it to me and my father had fallen in love with it and told me that he wanted me to perform it for a big concert he was doing in Denver the following month.

I was beside myself with anxiety over this request—which was really more like a demand. I had said I was not ready, but my father was insistent. I had the thing barely under my fingers but was a long way from having it in my heart and soul, which is where you have to have anything to perform it well. I felt trapped.

One afternoon when the rest of the family was away somewhere, which was unusual, I was ironing—one of my chores on Saturday. I ironed shirts and skirts and worried, and thought about how I might get out of this trap, and as I did so, I had a very new and, to me, wonderful idea: I decided I would kill myself.

I know that most people, when they have a problem, do not at once decide to commit suicide. Most of us who have depression do not wind up taking our lives, yet I was intrigued with this idea of self-murder. It took only a few moments after the idea came to my mind before I acted on it.

I went to the medicine cabinet in my parents' bathroom and looked eagerly about. My mother was as close to being a Christian Scientist as you could get without actually being one, and there was nothing in there but a few uninteresting-looking prescription bottles with God knew what in them, and an unopened bottle of aspirin. I tore open the aspirin bottle (it was easy, there were no

child-protection gizmos in those days) and threw hand-
fuls of the pills down my throat with huge swallows of
water. There were a hundred and fifty tablets and so it
took a while. I would iron for ten minutes, take a few
more pills, drink some water, and wait hopefully to fall
down dead, my problem solved. (Today it is understood
that large doses of aspirin can kill you.) The thought that
my father would regret his demands on me did in fact
cross my mind, which has always led me to believe there
is more to suicide in general than meets the eye.

Slowly, I began to feel lifted up and out of my problems, but then suddenly I was getting sick to my stomach.
I wanted to die but I certainly did not want to have to
throw up! It ruined the picture for me. I reached for the
phone and called the number of my best friend, Marcia.
But she was at a dance lesson, and her mother answered
the phone. Mrs. Pinto was a very sympathetic woman
and was married to a well-respected doctor. I told her
what I had done, and she said, "Put your finger down
your throat, get that stuff out of your stomach and I will
send Sherman over at once." I did as she told me.

When Dr. Pinto arrived he was very tender and kind.
He was with me when my mother arrived home and they
both hovered over me for a long time—Dr. Pinto with
great concern, my mother with a twist to her mouth that
told me she suspected me of somehow pulling one over
on her.

I know now that many people go into shock when a

suicide or an attempted suicide happens. And I understand that the reaction of people when someone they
love tries to kill themselves is part fury and part guilt, or
a combination of the two. And though I know today that
there are no guilty parties in suicide, the people caught
in the drama of a suicide experience many emotions and
are suddenly thrust into a situation to which there is no
perfect way to respond. There is no guidebook, no pat
answer to what triggered a daughter's attempt on her life.
The search for why is one that would involve a deeper
journey into places most people have no tools to handle.
Secrecy was the answer. And, of course, secrets can kill.

The result of my suicide attempt put to rest my father's
insistence that I play the Liszt at his big show and he
wrote me a letter in which he apologized for the demands
he put on me, for his perfectionism, for asking me to do
something I was sure I could not do. No one in the family ever mentioned it again. No therapist was called, no
intervention occurred. In those days, parents did not send
their suicidal kids to therapy. It seems that people thought
that someone who survived a suicide attempt had turned
a corner, had "gotten over it." Living was supposed to be
proof in that day and age that the problems were finished,
where for me, they were far from over.

They were just beginning.

CHAPTER 6

Hippocrates, Cornaro, Brillat-Savarin, Faxian, and William the Conqueror

Let food be thy medicine and medicine be thy food.

—HIPPOCRATES

More than two thousand years ago, Hippocrates wrote about clarity of mind and body with attention to food and exercise. He was a great believer in dietary measures in the treatment of disease and prescribed a "very slender, light diet during the crises stage of an acute illness, and a liquid diet during the treatment of fevers and wounds."

So before his time!

In 1558, Luigi Cornaro, a Venetian nobleman, first published the book we now know as *The Art of Living Long*. In the four treatises that comprise the book, begun in his early eighties and completed in his mid-nineties, Cornaro described having been saved from death by changing his diet. His food plan, recommended by a physician whom he consulted when he was deathly sick at the age of thirty-five, consisted of drinking no alcohol and eating less of everything and very little meat. "Intemperance," he says, "is the parent of gluttony," and "sober living is the offspring of abstemiousness." Cornaro's new diet, free of the alcohol and other foods that disagreed with him, consisted of a little protein (an egg perhaps), a vegetable soup made with tomatoes, grape juice (probably wine), and bread that he dipped in the soup. The result, a long and happy life, prompted him to write: "Having thus recovered my health, I began seriously to consider the power of temperance: if it had efficacy enough to subdue such grievous disorders as mine it must also have power to preserve me in health and strengthen my bad constitution. I therefore applied myself diligently to discover what kinds of food suited me best."

I sensed from his writing that Cornaro had found something that worked for his body as well as for his soul, his spirit, and his mind.

Jean Anthelme Brillat-Savarin, born in 1755, was a French lawyer and politician who was the mayor of Belley, a town on the border of Savoy and France. His opposition to the Jacobins during the French Revolution made him flee for his life to Switzerland in 1792 and then make his way to New York, where he survived by playing the violin. While playing the fiddle at a dinner, he met Thomas Jefferson and asked him how to cook a wild turkey. Jefferson, it is thought, instructed him in the American Thanksgiving cuisine.

After his cooking lessons and travels in Switzerland and America, Brillat-Savarin famously said, "Tell me what you eat, and I will tell you what you are." He returned to France and sat on the Supreme Court of Appeal in Paris until his death. During these years he spoke with many philosophers and physicians, and developed a course on obesity and its cure and was known for saying: "The destiny of nations depends on the manner in which they are fed."

I'll drink to that, and eat to it too.

Sometimes a spiritual journey has resulted in finding the answers on what to eat and what not to eat. For instance, there is the journey in the fifth century AD of the Chinese Buddhist monk Faxian, who made a pilgrimage from his home in China to India, walking hundreds of miles, looking for books about the Buddha. He had heard that more spiritually helpful books could be found about the great healer and prophet in India and decided he had to go. Four other monks joined him on his difficult journey. They visited shrines and searched for better manuscripts about Buddhism, which, like Christianity, has its sects, some very different from one another. There is even a Buddhist sect in Vietnam, where Buddhism is the third largest religion in the country, which calls itself the Cao Daists, whose followers believe in Christ, Buddha, and Victor Hugo.

Faxian's pilgrimage through India, which lasted many years, included the fording of wild and dangerous rivers, being practically stranded in a desert, and meeting up with both hospitable and inhospitable monks. Faxian found information other than what he was looking for—and isn't that often the case! We go seeking one thing, and around the corner is something that in time may very well change our lives. Faxian learned that "people . . . did not breed pigs or poultry or sell or consume any animal food." He found a predominance of vegetarianism, an idea he carried home along with the new books about the Buddha.

Abundance can also be an issue too—too much of a good thing. The popularity of dieting and problems with food seem to have been a front-page story since we discovered how to market, preserve, freeze, and present every conceivable kind of food at every season in the year—strawberries from the summer frozen for the winter, fruit from faraway countries easily purchased year-round from your local grocer. You name it, we have it. Even in earlier centuries, if you were royalty, you could probably get just about anything you wanted in the culinary department.

One of the most famous compulsive overeaters in history seems to be William the Conqueror, the first Norman king of England. He stood out for his power as a leader as well as for his girth, which during the years he was king became a real problem. In the year before his death, he used a liquid diet, consisting of beer and wine, to try to get back into his clothes and onto his horses.

For William the Conqueror, as for most of the royalty of that time, feasting was a dominant sport, right up there with fighting and ruling. William has been famous as someone who changed the course of English history, as well as one of the few monarchs we know of who went on a diet. We might as well call it the "William the Conqueror Diet," since many people who have tried to show the way to healthy eating use their own name to dignify their efforts. William's diet consisted of ale, beer, wine, and other "light" alcoholic beverages, which were the only liquids, except milk, that people drank in those days, as water was considered unhealthy.

There is reason to believe that the history of William's growing obesity did not just spring up in 1087 when he needed to lose weight to get back on his horse. His whole life had been leading to that moment.

The man who would be the king of England was born in 1028 in Normandy, France. His father, Duke Robert I of Normandy, was the descendant of Viking raiders, known for their fighting, feasting, and of course, as my Norwegian husband, Louis, reminds me, for their raping and pillaging sprees in Ireland, England, Scotland, and any other country they could sail to.

William's father was known as Robert the Magnificent and Robert the Devil. William's mother was Herleva Arlette de Falaise, the daughter of a tanner. She enchanted Robert with her lithe body and blond hair when he spied her from the roof of his castle tower. He sent a servant to invite her to his castle through the back door, as was a common practice. Herleva refused to report to the back door, arriving instead in style and making a grand entrance through the front door, dressed in fine silk and riding on a white stallion. Then she and Robert went at it and in no time at all, William was born, an illegitimate offspring with no real chance of inheriting his father's title.

William was nine when his father died and was afterward known among his family and friends as William the Bastard. He also managed, in spite of his illegitimacy, to be recognized as his father's heir and assume the title of Duke William of Normandy. He was brought up amid his father's cousins, who were fighting to depose him from his dukedom and were at war with opposing nobles.

In the 1050s William set his sights on the beautiful Matilda, the daughter of Count Baldwin V of Flanders. She first refused, saying she would never marry a man who was a bastard. William pursued her, hurrying to the town in which she lived. As Matilda walked to church he rode up to her (he, too, was on a white stallion), grabbed her by her braids, and threw her onto the dusty road. It seemed to work, for she changed her mind and agreed to marry him.

At the tables of the Norman dukes and duchesses, the meals they were served might still add up to twenty courses or more of every kind of fish, fowl, vegetable, soup, broth, delicacy, and dessert known to the courts of the privileged. They could choke a horse—or kill a king. (For example, take King Henry the VIII, who became woefully obese and suffered from diabetes, which, along with his extra pounds, probably killed him.) We must assume that the wedding feast was just that, food of all kinds from the entire culinary repertoire of both couples. The J. Paul Getty Museum in Los Angeles hosts what it calls "The King's Table: Recipes for a Medieval Feast," which consists of a "medieval coat of arms salad, marinated leeks in mustard vinaigrette, spinach and fava bean soup, grilled fish fillets with yellow sauce, French country sausage, rissoles [anything, meat or vegetable, in a pastry roll], spiced quince butter cake, spiced honey nut crunch, and spiced red wine."

This does not sound all that overwhelming until you realize that a royal wedding, and many royal meals, would begin at eleven in the morning and go on all day, with tasters for a king, and courses during the afternoon that might include hundreds of plates of food, variations on a theme, and all of them expected to be at least sampled. When he became the king of England, William would be facing a monumental cuisine at every meal in which the service might include, according to Kathryn Jones, the author of *For the Royal Table: Dining at the Palace,* 145 plates of food served during the first course alone. The service would probably include all the finest silver and gold but no glass and no forks. Meals would be served on fine linens that were embroidered with birds and exquisite scenes, but these were not courses as we know them; it was food piled high with obscene plentitude, meal after meal. One would have to have the stomach of a king, so to speak, to conquer them.

It was during this time that King Edward, childless and William's first cousin once removed, chose William as his heir to the English throne. However, Harold, Earl of Wessex, inherited the crown instead. He was at King Edward's side when the king died. Perhaps "being there" proved to be more than half the battle once again.

Harold was crowned king in Westminster Abbey in January 1066. In September, at the age of thirty-eight, Duke William mounted an army to invade England and claim what he and many others felt was his rightful inheritance. Calling out for King Harold to meet him in the fields of Hastings, William landed with his troops, prepared to enforce his claim to the English throne. Despite heavy losses, Duke William at last slew King Harold and was crowned the king of England, with of course the ensuing massive meals that went with the coronation.

The new king was thin, it was said, when he assumed the throne, and handsome, and he looked glorious on horseback. But as he grew older, King William began a serious fight with his weight. He was soon referred to as "robust and burly," and was observed to be uncomfortable with any reference to his weight.

William was not the only royal to try losing weight. Elizabeth von Wittelsbach, known as Sissi, empress consort of Austria, created a diet that would help her survive the mammoth meals served in the nineteenth-century Austrian court. She was constantly being looked at critically and knew she had to keep herself appealing and attractive to an increasingly jealous court and to a king with a wandering eye. She exercised, riding horses and often taking laxatives and eating only oranges. Dressed in ostrich-feather-trimmed gowns, she hung from pulleys that were strung up in her elegantly decorated rooms for stretching her limbs and working up a sweat. She became obsessed with her weight and turned to bulimia as well as exercise. Sissi did anything and everything, from starving and restricting her food intake, to eating only when she felt she was thin enough to deserve a meal. Sounds good to me!

In spite of his struggle with weight, King William sustained a long rule highlighted by many accomplishments, and he had a lasting effect on English history. Aside from becoming one of the fattest men in the history of royalty in England, he left an enduring impression on the world.

During his long reign William made a life's work of the collection of data on the holdings of English farming and business enterprises, an effort that resulted in the *Domesday Book,* in which all English businesses were listed and all taxes duly noted. But the fight to keep the weight off was getting him down and impacting his image as the great and handsome warrior who always appeared in public mounted on a magnificent stallion.

And of course the weight was creeping up every year, which is what happens to many of us in spite of our outward successes. His weight interfered with his image as well as his overall health. By the time he was in his fifties and living in France (while his son kept the court in London), King William was truly suffering.

At about this time, King Philip I of France started telling people that his cousin resembled a pregnant woman "about to give birth." King William took great offense at this comment. He determined to disprove his cousin and began a self-imposed diet of only liquids—which in those days meant English beer, or mead, as it was called, and perhaps wine. He locked himself in his French manor to drink himself thinner.

After some months of this regimen, William was able to mount his horse once more, though his stomach still hung over his belt. He set out for Philip's castle, mounted on a splendid steed, surrounded by his soldiers, to defeat the cousin who had insulted and made fun of him. In the battle with Philip's army at Mantes, William's horse shied and the pommel of the saddle drove into his abdomen, rupturing his intestines. He was taken to a nearby castle to recuperate, where his health worsened as an infection set in. Aware he was near death, William called for a priest and made a confession in which he admitted he had been a bad king. "I treated the [English] natives with severity, behaving like a raging lion, and was the cruel murderer of many thousands, both young and old, of this fair people."

King William died soon after his confession, but the humiliation of being overweight still pursued him when he had to be stuffed into his casket, and the prodding burst what was left of his innards, causing the mourners to flee the odors with great speed.

Perhaps William died as a result of the rage he felt at his royal cousin, who had the nerve to comment on his obesity. Perhaps, too, anger made him go into a battle for which he was ill-equipped, a fight he may have won in a younger, thinner body.

CHAPTER 7

Diets, Hunger, Starvation,
and Solutions

I lurched away from the table after a few hours feeling
like Elvis in Vegas—fat, drugged, and completely out
of it.

—ANTHONY BOURDAIN

It is an ironic fact of life that hunger affects millions of
people today. In the United States, starvation is at the
root of disease, pain, and even death. The need to con-
front the financial and social disorders that result in starvation in our abundant society is a great and urgent issue
and puts those of us with eating problems or who are
obese in a quandary; people are dying from starvation,
but they also die from eating disorders. The illnesses
underlying obesity, bulimia, anorexia, and purging can
be life-threatening, and we must work to help everyone

get the nourishing food they need as well as trying to understand eating disorders.

In May 2012 a report on the ABC news magazine *20/20* said that 100 million dieters, often on five or six diets a year, are spending $20 billion as a group—every year—to try to lose weight. Every year $500,000 to $3,000,000 is paid out to celebrity endorsers of weight-loss programs. Also in 2012, 220,000 people had major bariatric surgery (various procedures to decrease the size of the stomach) to lose weight. Over the past fifty years, I have been one of them, buying the books, signing up for the quick fix (everything but bariatric surgery), going for the gold in the Olympics of food restricting, playing games with my scales, my mirror, my clothing, my toilet bowl. It has been a disgusting, painful, costly, and, in many cases, useless journey for me, as it has for millions. Statistics from the National Institutes of Health say that obesity is on the rise along with eating disorders; the South Carolina Department of Mental Health says that one in two hundred women is bulimic. Studies show that in the overall area of mental health, more people who are suicidal also have eating disorders of one kind or another. The wrong food can cause depression. No wonder people continue to do anything and everything to find the right diet.

Obesity and starvation are both plagues in our country. We who have so much have illnesses often caused by too much of the wrong kind of food—starches, grains, sugar, and corn and corn syrup, a hidden ingredient in hundreds of foods, which can easily cause weight gain and addiction. We are also victims of hidden sugar, salt, and additives in formerly innocent foods—even breads—that once upon a time were free of GMOs and hidden ingredients that leave us wanting more, and more, and more, and more.

I am fortunate in that I have too much, rather than too little. I am grateful for that and I never forget that "there but for fortune go I," as Phil Ochs says in his great song. I also have the privilege of having a short list of what I try to do each day to keep my health and address my eating disorder. I have to be careful not to let perfectionism torment me—that can kill, too. We can do a little at a time. A friend of mine says that every time I judge myself harshly, I draw a drop of blood from my heart. So easy does it!

I meditate on a daily basis. This can be as simple as lighting a candle and closing the door and turning off the phone, sitting quietly in a cross-legged position and breathing in and out, counting the breaths, focusing on the point between my eyes. I say a favorite prayer for those I love, my nearest, dearest, and those I may be distanced from for some reason. I pray for peace in the world, and in my world. I might use the prayer of Saint Francis, he who loved animals and blessed and cared for the poor. Prayer and meditation dissolve negative feelings, lift the spirits, and connect me to something bigger in the universe. (I have a friend who thanks and requests help from the "Master of the Universe." She says while she is at it she might as well call on the biggest and the best!) Whatever your religious background, there is some way to find a spiritual connection that works for you. I love the sunsets and the ocean, which are often my stand-ins for a higher presence. Sometimes I think that's what they are there for.

For me exercise along with a diet free from sugar, grains, flour, and junk is the secret and my fountain of youth. I am told I look at least twenty years younger than my actual age. You can too. It is easy and does not have to involve expensive gyms or equipment. I run around the room at my hotel; I buy an inexpensive exercise tape and memorize a routine—it almost does not matter what the routine is as long as I do it consistently, twenty minutes, thirty minutes, forty minutes a day for a few days a week. It works.

I also drink a ton of water, probably sixty ounces or more a day. It is the source of life, the essence of fifty to sixty-five percent of our bodies. Sometimes when I feel exhausted and think I need a sugary drink, I am just dehydrated.

I usually sleep like a baby, unless I stay up late reading a book I can't put down. I often have to get up at 3:00 or 4:00 a.m. on the road, to catch those early flights so I can make connections to get all over the country. I sleep on planes, or in cars. Even so, I know I need more sleep than I get. Try to program a night in your week, or two nights, where you actually get more sleep than you think you need. For me, it often sparks up my attitude, my courage, my appreciation for life, and my tolerance of other's faults, as well as my own.

Music is healing—and I'm not saying that just because I make my living performing it. I listen to other singers, great musicians, classical, pop, country, and traditional. I go to a concert, go out dancing, or stay in and play some good old rock and roll. Dance with your own stars, and you will feel better.

I eat like a king and truly enjoy every meal. Celebrate your part in creating these wonderful meals. Use your imagination, or do as I do, have the same thing for breakfast, lunch, and dinner. Keep it simple or spice it up with something amazing. Diabetes is a worldwide problem and sugar is the main culprit. Taking sugar, grains, flour, wheat, and bad carbs out of our food plans can make a dramatic change—we lose weight, we gain beauty, we come for the vanity and stay for the sanity. We are reborn.

Getting on the right course of foods for your body, mind, and spirit can turn back the restless hands of time. You will look younger, have more energy, love your life more, enjoy your kids and grandkids. You might even love or at least tolerate your trials, know you can get through them more easily, and count them, in some cases, as privileges. It is a privilege for many of us to live on the planet, warts, wars, wonders, and all.

I know from years of painful experience that a food illness might not show in the body. Heavier than I wanted to be, I was always trying to lose the pounds. Having lost the pounds, I was always crazy to keep them off at any cost. That meant that the illness was in control until I could find a way of peace and tranquillity that did not involve fighting food all day long, every day. It is not the weight but the illness—one as devastating and dangerous as alcoholism or drug addiction, and even more misunderstood—that might result in death.

So now that there is so much junk available everywhere—in those little stores on the roads and in the big markets in the cities—made with sugar, flour, grains, and wheat, how do we food addicts, compulsive overeaters, bulimics, bingers, and purgers who cannot eat comfortably figure out how to avoid the food and overcome our cravings?

If we take the numbers of obese and overweight people in the country today (34.9 percent, or 79 million, according to the Centers for Disease Control in 2014), it would appear that millions of people are, like me, allergic to the foods that cause these cravings. And these are the foods that are responsible for heart disease, stroke, type 2 diabetes, certain kinds of cancer, and other causes of preventable death. It's worth remembering the science: At 98.6 degrees, grains, sugar, flour, wheat, and corn turn into alcohol, which can set off the craving in the body and the mind—just as it causes the urge in alcoholics to drink. Are the people who say they are not allergic to these foods still having problems with their weight?

Perhaps it is just the foods themselves that are wrong for us. Alcohol, flour, sugar, grains, potatoes, corn, and junk food are not necessary for a proper diet. And since we are looking at statistics, I wonder if the group of people who are actually allergic to these foods is much larger than we think.

That stores are full of the foods that many of us are allergic to always gives me pause and leaves me with questions about why we are drawn to these toxic foods. Many have asked these questions. Before the twentieth century people were not faced with fast-food vendors and sugar, sugar, sugar around every corner. Yet many of them were consumed with the thoughts of food, and many of them had to fight the inner demons we fight today.

But there is a solution. Don't walk away five minutes before the miracle.

CHAPTER 8

MY JOURNEY

Teenage Years

Too much of a good thing can be—wonderful!

—MAE WEST

In my thin youth in Colorado, after the suicide attempt and in spite of my addiction to sugar and my drinking, I was blissfully unaware for the most part of my own emotional instability. There were troubles brewing— putting on weight and losing it. I never really noticed how much I weighed. My clothes fit me. Until I was about fifteen, though I had already started to drink, I did not show outward signs of addiction. Later there were more serious health complications, combined in my case with undereating and restricting (eating less at each meal than a normal person) and bulimia, which caused my bones to suffer, my menstrual period to all but stop, and my general health to deteriorate. As I grew past my teenage angst, I never stopped looking for a solution, trying diets, reading books, finally going to weekly therapy— for thirty years.

At sixteen I was being a typical teenager, dating, necking with my boyfriends in the movies—and eating anything and everything I wanted: Jujubes, popcorn, Necco Wafers, chocolate fudge, and Rice Krispies squares, the pies and cakes my mother baked, chocolate-covered cherries. Because I had a little money from babysitting, doing chores at home, and teaching piano to a few young students, I could now buy hamburgers at the drive-in, where the waitresses were often on roller skates, and delicious chocolate milk shakes of which I usually ordered two.

I did not gain weight during my teenage years, or think much about it. I was, as usual, running all the time, from my classes at Smiley Junior High and then at East High School to working on my "Little Red Riding Hood" shows with my friends, Marcia and Carol. I composed themes for the Grandmother, the Wolf, and the Woodsman and played them on the piano while Marcia and Carol danced the story. We finagled our friends Peggy and Susan into taking the parts of the other characters, and soon we were performing at the Lions, Elks, Rotary, and Kiwanis clubs, the PTA Convention, and East High School. We even performed at Lowry Air Force Base and Fitzsimons Army Hospital just outside of Denver. We were planning on taking our show to Las Vegas.

Eventually our fairy tale ran its course and we knew we needed another story. I was leaning toward "Snow White and the Seven Dwarfs." We had even started pulling in ringers for the dwarfs from our high-school buddies.

At the time I was still practicing the piano every afternoon. I was learning the Rachmaninoff Concerto no. 2 on the Baldwin grand that my parents had bought me when I was eleven. Antonia Brico had promised me I would play the Rachmaninoff with her orchestra as soon as I was ready. She knew I "fooled around," as she put it, with other kinds of music but had always believed I would choose the piano and the classics in the end.

Neither of us knew I was about to break her heart.

One Saturday I was preparing, as usual, to practice. To this day I don't know what prompted me to turn on our Emerson radio in the dining room. It was my luck that in Denver in 1954, some adventurous, brave disc jockey was unaware that he was about to change the life of a fifteen-year-old. That afternoon I heard "The Gypsy Rover" sung by Elton Hayes from the sound track of Alan Ladd's movie *The Black Knight*. I fell head over heels in love when I heard the song. That afternoon would turn me into a folksinger, as though I had been touched, as were many of my fairy-tale heroines, by a magic wand.

I raced out on Monday after school to Wells Music, Denver's premier music store, where I bought the recording of "The Gypsy Rover." I told Carol and Marcia I had found our next story, and in a few days we were practicing the song, which we had to learn from the radio since I had sat on the vinyl record and cracked it into a hundred pieces.

On a subsequent Saturday afternoon I again found the same disc jockey. He brought me another revelation, for among his menu of Frank Sinatra and Percy Faith recordings, he played Jo Stafford singing "Barbara Allen," from Stafford's 1950 album, *American Folk Songs*. Somehow this disc jockey had led me to the next stage of my career.

I soon convinced my father to find me a guitar (he rented it, being an optimist) and I slowly learned to play, listening to other folk songs I loved, fighting to get my calluses to stop bleeding. After learning two traditional songs, I was on my way, leaving Mozart, Rachmaninoff, and Bach in the dust. I did not weep, I was in ecstasy. I would leave the weeping to Brico, who made up for my lack of tears.

And now, as before, there was always the food and lots of sugar, which I would have chosen to live on exclusively if I could. I also loved to eat all kinds of other wonderful things. The hamburgers at the local diner were a dream, with ketchup and grilled onions and that green relish that I have never tasted the likes of since, all melting in your mouth. Alcohol was now part of my life as well, and I would have a beer at home with my family—or three fingers of good whiskey or bourbon when my father was pouring and in his cups. I began to cook at home and make things I wanted, learning from my mother how to make Toll House cookies, sifting flour for cakes, frosting sugar cookies for Christmas and decorating them with a baker's twist, and licking all the bowls. I had chocolate bars in my lunches and always something sugary instead of fruit for desserts. I drank like a fish when I got the chance. I started smoking, bumming cigarettes at first, choking and coughing, and finally buying my own Camels. The best diner in Denver was across from East High School, and there my friends and I smoked cigarettes and talked about Albert Camus and the war in Algeria. We knew we were going to change the world, stop the violence, make a difference.

In that year of my heady first encounter with folk songs, acquiring a guitar and slumming in the Denver Folklore Center on East Seventeenth Avenue, buying records and learning songs, I also met Lingo the Drifter. He was a singer and troubadour who had a radio show in Denver and became a fan and friend of my father's. Daddy had a show on another radio station, and Lingo at first introduced himself to Daddy, and then would come to our house and sing to me and my family, playing his old beat-up Martin guitar. He was not of the world that my dad's music inhabited—Rodgers and Hart, George Gershwin—though he and my dad had similar political views. They both thought everybody, from the president on down, was lying. It was my first exposure to another conspiracy theorist outside our family enclave.

My father's whiskey flowed in the evenings when

Lingo visited and I was allowed a drink or two (or maybe more, if my mother was not looking).

Lingo was a character from a storybook, and in those innocent days of short hair, Brooks Brothers shirts, khaki pants, and poodle skirts, he would rock my world in a way that nothing else had. His clothes and his songs were from the Woody Guthrie and Pete Seeger catalog, his guitar slung around his neck with an old leather strap, his hat floppy, half Stetson and half train conductor, battered and worn, with a pine sprig sticking out of the band. He wore buckskin trousers and a leather shirt with a bolo tie. Soon I was making my way to gatherings at Lingo's cabin on Lookout Mountain, where I sat around on a Saturday night with other folkies with their long hair, sandals, funky clothes, long beaded necklaces: girls with beautiful yearning eyes and dark makeup, boys with slender hands and thin waistlines, waifs with lots of turquoise and beaded moccasins, refugees from high schools in Denver and little towns in the mountains, all looking for love in the songs of Woody and Pete, longing to change the world and stop the wars. We sat cross-legged on the puncheon floor (sliced pine logs upended and cut evenly to make a smooth surface) of Lingo's cabin, exclaiming about Indochina (the French were already losing) and exchanging versions of "Barbara Allen" and "Los Quarto Generales" from the Spanish Civil War. We downed overflowing cups of home brew and smoked weed (which I hated—even then it made me paranoid) and ate sweet desserts and Lingo's homemade borscht. Home brew was on tap at the folk-music parties I went to in Denver as well.

And oh, the songs! I learned there was an entire universe filled with beauty and melody, history and lyrics, magic. In those nights at Lookout Mountain, Lingo the Drifter taught me "This Land Is Your Land," and Mart Hoffman, a young singer from Colorado, sang, in his beautiful, lilting voice, "Deportees" and "Pastures of Plenty"; Dick Barker, a junior at Colorado University and a rancher with a musky, sexy voice, sang cowboy songs like "Dolores" and "The Lavender Cowboy" and "I Ride an Old Paint." They are all gone now except in my dreams.

I started buying the records of Pete Seeger and Bob Gibson, Josh White and the Clancy Brothers at the Denver Folklore Center, where all the young folksingers gathered. I was hooked for life.

At home, as I sat down to practice Rachmaninoff and Debussy (which I was still playing every day), I began to feel that practicing was interfering with my drinking, whereas the guitar and the folk songs and the parties on Lookout Mountain seemed to blend in perfectly.

I spent hours now haunting the record stores and digging through the files at Wells Music for Woody Guthrie and Pete Seeger songbooks, the Child Ballads collections of ancient and even more ancient songs, the recordings of Ewan MacColl and Peggy Seeger. At home at the Baldwin grand, I was still practicing the classics, Mozart and Chopin and Czerny, doing my Hanon exercises. Now, because of my increasing love of and interest in folk music, I began to realize my heart was torn. I began to feel like a spy in the house of Beethoven.

I spent the summer when I was fifteen working at Sportsland Valley Guest Ranch, where I rode horses, cleaned cabins, sang "Barbara Allen" while I played the piano in the lodge, and fell in love with my husband-to-be. Peter Taylor was two years older than I, loved the songs I sang, was from Denver but was at school in Boulder where he was a sophomore at the University of Colorado. I had been teaching his sister, Hadley, piano for a couple of years, and she had finally arranged to have us meet. At the lodge where Peter had worked in previous summers and Hadley and I were both cleaning cabins and waiting tables, Peter and I spent a delicious few weeks in the mountains, and we were bonded before the end of August. He headed back to university and I headed back to East High, and then, that autumn, everything was romance and folk music and being a teenager.

September, with school back in session, I put my music books under my arm on a Monday afternoon, got on the Colfax bus and rode downtown to my biweekly lesson at Brico's studio on Seventeenth Street. There, in her stone-hewn studio, between the Steinway pianos, the portraits of Beethoven, Bach, Brahms, and Casals, I faced the music at last. In a shaking voice, near tears, I told my teacher I was not going to play Rachmaninoff with her orchestra but was going to devote myself to "Barbara Allen," "The Gypsy Rover," "Pretty Saro," and "The Streets of Laredo." "I am going to be a folksinger," I told this pioneer of the world of classical music, the woman warrior who had broken all the rules to do what she loved, when everyone said it could never happen.

After many tears, I left Brico's studio for good. I have never stopped practicing, and when I started writing my own songs, I have always composed those songs on the piano. But I have never looked back and I have never regretted the musical passion that changed my life.

High school was a blur of playing folk songs at the school shows, singing "The Gypsy Rover" while Carol and Marcia danced the story, living out my fantasies, and dating Peter when he came down from Boulder. My weight, and my concern for how I looked and what I ate, felt like a hazy dream. I was happy, I was certainly not fat, and I was playing the music that would make my life what it is today. And I was in love, and love is one of the best dieting tools ever to come down the pike.

Peter and I saw each other every time we could. When I graduated from high school I went off for a year to MacMurray, a small Presbyterian college in the Midwest. I didn't drink, as drinking at the school was a no-no, but I ate. I was turning a corner into the world of dieting and bingeing, watching the calories and eating sparingly one day, and the next day gorging myself on anything, from the boxes of sweets my mother sent week after week to the potatoes served at lunch in the cafeteria.

I could never tell when the urge would come along. My lover was far away, and the love-fever diet was burning low from lack of day-to-day fuel. I was all appetite all the time and smoking cigarettes like a fiend, hoping they would curb my appetite. I was struggling every day not to eat what was in the sugar-laden packages from home. I had been walking on the edge of a cliff for years and now was in danger of going over. I felt as though I were mortally wounded. I was gaining weight and terribly homesick.

On a visit to Denver during March vacation in 1958, Peter and I went on a ski trip to Georgetown, in the mountains west of Denver. We checked into a rustic hotel after a day of skiing. In our hotel room, shy but determined, we spent a night together for the first time. Those were not the days of easy access for unwed couples to rooms and beds of their own—and when I returned to school on the train from Denver a few weeks later, I realized I was pregnant. I was beside myself, but as soon as I got back to Denver at the end of May, Peter and I decided we were going to get married. We had been devoted to each other for three years by then. It was the most natural thing in the world for us. I was eighteen and pregnant, and as soon as we agreed that we were together and would have our baby, I relaxed and fell eagerly into the work of being pregnant—which meant gaining twenty-five pounds almost at once.

I found that once I started eating, as with alcohol, I could not stop.

CHAPTER 9

LIVES OF THE DIET GURUS

William Banting

> We shall not cease from exploration
> And the end of all our exploring
> Will be to arrive where we started
> And know the place for the first time.

> —T. S. ELIOT

It seems that only people who have problems with food write books about and create diets for losing weight. They are looking for a solution for themselves and then writing about their successes. There are hundreds, possibly thousands of weight-loss books that have come out since the time of Gayelord Hauser, but everyone in the field of the popular diet in the twentieth century—Robert Atkins, Blake F. Donaldson, Herman Tarnower, Adelle Davis, and Dr. Oz, even Hauser—owes allegiance to William Banting.

Banting's clients (are the deceased still clients?) were Edward V and Edward VI, Queen Victoria, Prince Albert, Prince Leopold, King George IV, the Duke of Gloucester, and the Duke of Wellington, as well as many other royal families in nineteenth-century England. As the funeral director to the Royal House, he led a high-profile life, often seen among heads of state who were appearing at court. He and his family were welcomed into the Victorian homes of the great and famous.

As a young man, Banting had weighed 152 pounds, but by 1862, when he was in his sixties, he was up to 202 pounds. The weight gain was causing him to suffer tremendous discomfort. He had boils and could climb a flight of stairs only by going up backwards, a solution he had arrived at as he gained weight. He was humiliated by his condition, unable to breathe and walk easily under the best of circumstances. Then a painful earache had brought him to his knees. Banting was in despair. "I could not stoop to tie my shoes . . . nor attend to the little offices humanity requires, without considerable pain and difficulty, which only the corpulent can understand."

In his youth, he had been a thin man able to scull and run with the best of his peers, but now he was in his sixties and found that even helping carry coffins in the ceremonies at Westminster and the other churches in London had become next to impossible. Some things he could probably manage—signing letters of sympathy to kings and queens, gazing into a bier. Banting did not think a man like himself—rich and successful—should have to put up with this pain. He tried everything to soothe his earache, applying mustard packs that his wife recommended, taking the awful-tasting bitters that his brother-in-law suggested, alternating placing his head on a hot pad and then a cold pad, and lying with his feet up, which was virtually impossible given his weight. But nothing worked. Banting's usual doctor was no longer seeing patients, so he went to a new physician, Dr. William Harvey, who would change Banting's life.

Harvey was known as one of the great men of science, and he was the first doctor on record to use "blind experiments" to ensure objectivity in his scientific observations. Louis-Napoléon met Harvey in 1864 and set him up with his own laboratory and professorship at the Académie française in Paris, where he was awarded a doctorate from the Académie des sciences. Harvey regularly traveled between London and Paris and, at the time Banting went to see him, had just returned from France, where he had heard a lecture by Claude Bernard, the famous physician and physiologist. Bernard had discussed sugar and its relationship to the liver and to diabetes.

After examining Banting, Harvey decided that the body fat on his neck was causing the earache. He gave his patient a prescription that was a diet of meat, with little sugar, bread, or beer. Banting could have up to six ounces of bacon, beef, mutton, venison, kidneys, fish, or any form of poultry, and plenty of tea without milk or sugar. He could have "fruit of the pastry" but not the pastry; any vegetables but potatoes; up to three glasses of Sherry a day; and one ounce of dry toast.

After a year of following Harvey's advice, Banting lost forty-six pounds and inches off his waist, regained his hearing, and could get up and down stairs again.

Banting was now a true convert, a man who had been reborn into a new and healthy body. He was back to 154 pounds and so thrilled with his weight loss that he wanted to share his new knowledge with the world. He wrote and then published *Letter on Corpulence: Addressed to the Public* to spread the good word of the miracle. Banting's pamphlet, printed in many editions over the past hundred and fifty years, tells the story of a formerly overweight sixty-five-year-old man, fat, sick, and discouraged, whose life was now "more luxurious and liberal . . . more healthful."

The term "Banting" was used for decades in the U.K. for dieting, and in Sweden it became the name for slimming or dieting. Banting's publication has probably influenced contemporary physicians and scientists who are investigating a low-carb diet as people began to read about the "Banting" diet. Gary Taubes, in his 2007 book, *Good Calories, Bad Calories,* claims that Banting was not really on a low-carb diet but on a lower calorie diet. Who cared? Finally, somebody was actually talking about being fat. Really talking, in print, about all the things many people were worried about—not getting into their clothes, having terrible health problems, losing friends, jobs, respect. It was about time to think about these things, talk about them, and Banting led the way.

The British weekly magazine *Punch* even printed a poem about Banting's journey:

If you wish to grow thinner diminish your dinner
And take to light claret instead of pale ale;
Look down with an utter contempt upon butter
And never touch bread till it's toasted—not stale.

"I've done it," said brave Mr. Banting,
And so may each overfed Briton,
If he'd only adapt resolution severe
And avoid—if he would not grow fatter and fatter,
All bread, butter, sugar, milk, 'taters and beer.

MY JOURNEY

The Late Fifties and the Sixties

Eat breakfast like a king, lunch like a prince, and dinner like a pauper.

—ADELLE DAVIS

I came back from MacMurray College in May 1958 already a couple of months pregnant. Peter and I would marry as soon as we could and at once began life as a couple and headed for the mountains we both loved. We had been practically engaged for two years by then, and Holden and Ann Bowler, my godfather and his wife, invited us to stay as long as we liked at their cabin in the mountains above Estes Park. We headed to the mountains, our backpacks and gear stuffed into Peter's Chevy station wagon, unloaded everything at Holden and Ann's cabin, and started looking for summer jobs in Estes Park as well as making plans for our wedding. We had the blood tests and the marriage license; all we needed was a judge and a way to make some kind of living.

We were lucky enough to find work right away, running an old lodge at Fern Lake, an idyllic hostel on a nine-mile hike between Bear Lake and Moraine Park. Jim Bishop, whose mother had built Bear Lake Lodge as well as Fern Lake Lodge, told us his chef would teach me how to bake bread on a woodstove and would make sure Peter knew how to chop wood and keep the spring running. We would serve lunch to hikers. We would live in a pine-hewn cabin by the side of the crystal lake. The pay was $300 for the entire summer. We were ecstatic.

After a couple of days at Bear Lake Lodge, sleeping in a loft with the smells of pine from the forest and beef stew from the kitchen and getting to know the ropes, Peter and I slung our fifty-pound packs on our backs and headed up the trail to Fern Lake Lodge.

It was about four and a half miles, straight up from 9,000 to 11,000 feet. The lodge we found in this breathtaking wilderness of pines, sun, shadow, and crystal-clear water had no electricity, no running water, just a telephone and some of the most beautiful of the Rocky Mountains in our front yard. We settled in, giddy at our good fortune. This would be our wedding celebration and our honeymoon all in one glorious setting, during that summer. Our best, we would think as we looked back on it in the years to come.

Our supplies arrived once a week by packhorse and

included Mars bars, Oh Henrys, Necco Wafers, and Almond Joys (for the guests); a bottle of Jim Beam (for us); tortillas, avocados, ground beef, cheese, Spam, peanut butter, jelly, flour, rice, and big cans of peaches, cherries, and apples; and sugar for the pies and for the wine that we brewed from the leftover juice of the cherries, apples, and peaches. I baked single buns on the woodstove for the sandwiches on which we served sliced Spam or grilled hamburger patties and sliced cheese.

Our only connection with the world was a working telephone on which I would call my parents once a week. Peter manned the woodcutting and the pipes that brought us the clear, crystal water from the mountain springs. I quickly learned to bake bread on the woodstove as well, one of three industrial-size stoves in the sixty-year-old kitchen, which was also supplied with decades of cutlery, baking pans, metal saucepans for simmering and boiling and stewing, pans for roasting, spitting, and sautéing. Hot water made its way from a radiator strapped to the back of the big fireplace in the main lodge, heated by the fire and sent through pipes to the kitchen. For showers, more hot water ran through those pipes to a washtub punched with holes and hung upside down above our heads and then flowed into a large bucket on the floor. By lunchtime, as we heard the voices of our guests calling from the trail, we would be sparkling clean and ready to serve.

We knew we had arrived in heaven.

It was a sparse menu, but up there, after having climbed

from 9,000 to 11,000 feet, weary, hungry, and thirsty, those hikers found a haven. They would linger and rest for a few hours, listening to the girl with long hair, the budding folksinger, who would have changed out of an apron to a pair of Levi's (that became tighter and tighter as the summer wore on and I gained weight from the pregnancy) and a cotton shirt (shirttails out as the summer progressed) and would play the guitar and sing for them: "Ten Thousand Goddam Cattle," "Cool Water," "Barbara Allen," and "This Land Is Your Land." Out on the deck of our lodge, the hikers basked in the sun as their noses burned and they watched a red fox, the occasional deer, or a Rocky Mountain Martin come down to drink from our pristine lake. Then they were off, down the other side to Moraine Park, picked up by a cousin or a wife or a brother-in-law who had brought the car around from the Bear Lake side instead of making the hike to our aerie at the top of the trail, our mountain haven in the Rockies.

MENU FOR LUNCH AT FERN LAKE LODGE

Sandwiches of cheese, Spam, or hamburger on
   homemade rolls with grilled onions, tomatoes,
   and mustard
Homemade cherry and apple pies
Raspberry iced tea

Regular iced tea

Spring water

Oh Henrys, Mars bars, Almond Joys, Oreos (plenty
   of sugar!)

Oranges

Apples

When my family came to Fern Lake for a weekend,
my father followed Mom up the trail to the deliciously
cool and clear Dream Lake and then Fern Lake, like
pools of silver at the foot of the peaks and pine trees. He
grabbed on to a pine bough that Mom held and followed
her, as steady-footed as any sighted hiker out for a summer mountain adventure. At the lodge, we housed my
parents and siblings in one of the cabins—there were a
dozen, all equipped with feather beds, quilts, and potbel-
lied stoves. We ate in the lodge in front of a blazing fire
(it was cold up there at night, even in the summer). My
mother told me she was surprised I did not have morning
sickness (I never had any nausea when I was pregnant)
and that most people would be sick from having to cook
for all those hikers. It never bothered me a bit, and I
was as active pregnant as I ever was, the running-around
instinct in full swing.

Peter and I were married on a weekend in July, in
Loveland. We hiked down to Moraine Park where our
friend Judy Holland awaited us; we borrowed her pickup
and she took care of the lodge, the hikers, the pies and

sandwiches, which I had left ready and waiting for our guests. The judge's wife and his secretary were witnesses to our marriage at the courthouse, and then we rushed back up the mountain, legally bound.

This summer in the mountains, under the stars and moon, and under the sun and in the sparkle of the lake at our feet, was something unique and we knew it. We were happy, and at the end of the summer, our packs were lighter and our hearts were sick as we hiked back down to civilization. I carried the same pack on my back that I had brought up the mountain, followed by the pack-horse with my guitar and the rest of our meager possessions. The hike was one I would take in future years many times, always joyful to get back to our mountain retreat on the shores of Fern Lake.

I was now five months pregnant. Back in Boulder, Peter returned to school to get his master's degree. After twenty-eight hours of labor, I gave birth to my beautiful redheaded baby, Clark Collin Taylor, on January 8, 1959. He weighed nine pounds and two ounces, and he and I stayed in the hospital for ten days. It was a Seventh-day Adventist hospital, where they served no coffee and no meat, so I was in detox from caffeine as well as booze.

After a few weeks of being at home with the baby in our basement apartment in Boulder, I got a job filing papers at the University of Colorado's administration offices. One night during a blizzard, Peter suggested I find a job doing "something you know how to do, like sing!" I called my dad and got a recommendation for an audition at Michael's Pub in Boulder, an Italian restaurant and college hangout where pizza, 3.2 beer, and barbershop quartets were the usual fare. I was a hit, and Mike Besesi hired me at a hundred dollars a week—a fortune in those days—and all the beer and pizza I could handle. I went to work at Michael's Pub and for many weeks that spring made a living that enabled me to support my husband and new baby.

At Michael's Pub, I continued the passion that had started when I found those first folk songs when I was fifteen, and as those weeks and months went by, my career took off like a dream come true. The suffering also began, starting with a deep anxiety that made it hard for me to sleep and an increased need to drink more and to find ways to deal with what I thought was a form of mental illness. For most of my twenties and thirties, I was afraid much of the time, fearing I was crazy and would have to be locked up sometime in the future.

But while I was performing my anxieties and fears disappeared; the music gave me peace of mind, the melodies and lyrics gave me wings. And the pain of the increase in my drinking and the growing evidence that I had a problem with food did not seem to impact my career. From the first time I went to Michael's Pub in my tights and red top, my hair in a short, spiky cut, I have never stopped loving to perform and to learn new songs. Possibly it is because of all the years of preparation, the hours of study, and the pressures of living in a big family with many responsibilities. Performing felt natural to me.

Peter, Clark, and I moved from Boulder to Central City in the summer of 1959. I worked at the Gilded Garter on the bill with a rock-and-roll singer named Donna St. Thomas. I also worked as a waitress during the day at the Teller House restaurant. Peter, who was still studying for his degree, took care of Clark at night, and when August came the three of us moved back to Boulder, this time to a little cabin next to Boulder Creek.

It was very romantic, Peter in school studying English lit and me spending my days with my beautiful baby and going to Denver at night to work at the Exodus, a new club that featured folk artists. My eating habits were somewhat curtailed because I didn't really have time for bingeing, but I certainly drank more than anyone else around and probably drove drunk more nights than I would like to admit. I was in the big-time, opening for Josh White, the Tarriers, Bob Gibson, and Don Crawford. I got to know them and learned more each night about my craft and my calling. To get to work at the Exodus I drove an hour and a half on the Denver Boulder turnpike five nights a week, but it was a great experience and I was making good money: $110 a week, up from $100 at Michael's Pub.

In February Peter and I went skiing at Winter Park with his brother Gary and Gary's fiancée, Minky Goodman. I took a tumble that shattered my right leg—a double spiral fracture that put me in the hospital for two weeks. Demerol every four hours for a week, and when I came home I had a cast from my toes to my hip. I began to swing around on crutches in no time and was back working at the Exodus when I got a call from the Gate of Horn in Chicago, asking me to open for six weeks in the coming summer for a singer named Will Holt.

Peter and I had been offered another kind of job for the summer—the fire watch at Twin Sisters in Rocky Mountain National Park. It was a hard choice, but I knew I could not take the fire watch with my leg in a cast. So we decided to move to Chicago. About the same time Peter received a teaching fellowship at the University of Connecticut in Storrs. It meant our lives were changing dramatically, and all at once. We packed for Chicago and sent the rest of our things to the East Coast. Peter rented a house on a hill on a farm near the university, and we were on our way.

I would look back sometimes and think that I could have had a career with the National Park Service—Peter could have become a Longs Peak ranger, like our friends John Clark and Erny Kuncl. But it was not to be; the dice had already been rolled when I heard "The Gypsy Rover" on the radio. I could not go back, I had to go forward.

Albert Grossman, a Chicago native with big ideas and a love of folk artists, founded the Gate of Horn in 1956. His first client was Bob Gibson, who became a star after playing an eleven-month gig at the club in 1958. By the end of those months Gibson had made his name, and so had the Gate of Horn, a hundred-seat room in the basement of the Rice Hotel on North Dearborn. It was a rough-hewn, simply furnished, wooden-floored, small-stage harbor for folksingers from all over the world, and became a hot club in the folk quartet of Los Angeles, New York, San Francisco, and Chicago. Everyone I had known from records and rumors, from Sonny Terry and Brownie McGhee to the Clancy Brothers and Tommy Makem, Theo Bikel, Josh White, Odetta, and even Lenny Bruce, had worked at the Gate.

I was introduced to speed at the Gate—little white pills that would get me through one more night of singing. I was working six nights a week, three shows a night. I drank absinthe between shows, and ate whatever and whenever I wanted. I gained weight in spite of the amphetamines, but Peter and I had a wonderful apartment on the North Side, and I would come home at midnight to my baby and my husband and could sleep late.

By the fall of 1960, we had moved to Storrs, Connecticut, and Peter was teaching and I was touring. By 1961, I was doing two-week stretches at Gerde's Folk City in New York and playing other clubs around the country. I had a record contract with Elektra, a manager (Harold Leventhal), and bookings from New York to California and in clubs and on concert stages around the country.

My life in the world of music has always been peopled with gallant and gifted souls, from Bob Dylan to Joan Baez, from Pete Seeger to Joni Mitchell, from Sandy Denny to Arlo Guthrie, from Jim Morrison to Al Kooper. From the famous to the infamous. All through these early years, I laid the foundation for a lifetime career, studying, singing, touring, and making albums.

My illnesses—the food addiction and the alcoholism—grew and thrived like weeds in a sunny garden. My career was also growing, blossoming, carrying me to places I never imagined I would see.

All the while, there were sexual searches aided by drugs and alcohol that fueled my emotional and physical enlightenment, which was helped along by reading *The Story of O* and doing what came naturally. I had to find a way to let down after the high of performing, after a night of catching up on the levels of alcohol and food it took to keep the heart happy. And although one-night stands accompanied by loneliness were common among my compatriots and myself, falling in love was a no-no. I should have known it was bound to happen.

I was away from home too much, working, traveling from town to town, coming home to the rolling countryside in Storrs. With my husband and my growing baby, I would hunker down for a few days of sanity, but was drinking too much, eating too much, getting into alcohol- and sugar-fueled arguments with Peter, and then hugging my son and going back out on the road.

It was bad enough that in the spring of 1962 Peter and I talked about me "getting off the road." We talked and thought about it for a day and a half, and then realized with my decreased income we would have to move into university housing (God forbid). We had gotten accustomed to the money I made—enough to allow us to live in our rented farmhouse in the countryside, with cows and flowers, the woods as our backyard, fireflies at night in the fragrant grasses, walks in the meadows up above our red barn, where I could commune with the land for a few days between smoke-filled clubs and three shows a night, six days a week, and Peter could have a retreat from teaching English literature to freshmen at the university. At home in the Connecticut hills I would cook happily, drink with my husband, and devour sweet things that I shouldn't have. I was keeping the weight in line with my own emotional misery and at times with pills and restricting.

We couldn't imagine giving that up, and soon I had accepted another month-long engagement at the Gate of Horn, where there were long nights of drinking and singing and long days of sleeping late and recovering from the long nights.

My marriage had begun to fall apart and I had what I know now was probably a nervous breakdown, or perhaps the beginning of my bottoming out on booze and food and too much work and too little time with my family. Finally, with all this success, I began having my first affair, hard to handle under the best of circumstances. I finally found the one "without whom I could not live." Driven by my illnesses, I was willing to throw it all out—the marriage, the life of a professor's wife, the calm and security of a home in the hills of Connecticut.

My lover, a musician with whom I was making an album, would drop into a town where I was working for a day or so now and then, but I was filled by that time with guilt and anxiety, loathing who I was becoming. I didn't like myself, and didn't trust myself, with my work, my husband, my son, or even my lover.

All of them were getting short shrift—and so was I.

CHAPTER 11

Jean Nidetch and Weight Watchers

> The food you eat can be either the safest and most
> powerful form of medicine or the slowest form of poison.
>
> —ANN WIGMORE

In 1961, while I was living in Connecticut with Peter and Clark, a woman named Jean Nidetch started a journey that would change her life as well as the lives of millions of others.

Nidetch was blond, five foot four, and weighed 214 pounds. In the spring of 1961 she wore a size 44 dress. She was a mother—her first child had died in infancy and her son, David, was nine. She was married to Marty, who was also overweight.

Born in Brooklyn, she briefly attended City College in New York City. Nidetch had been making a living for years in various jobs, once working for Man o' War Publishing Company writing tips for horse races until Mayor La Guardia clamped down on betting. While working at the IRS, she met and married Marty Nidetch.

In her 2010 autobiography, Nidetch described herself at this time in her life as "an overweight woman, with an overweight husband, surrounded by overweight friends." She had been overweight all of her childhood and adult life, and spoke of herself as being "desperate" again, as she had been on and off all the diets of that time, and none of them worked.

One day one of her old friends, astonished at Nidetch's size, asked her, smiling in what she thought was shared happiness, if she was pregnant again. Within a few days Jean enrolled in the New York City Department of Health Obesity Clinic. It is amazing to me that there was such a thing in 1961, a free program with a weight-loss plan, pamphlets with instructions on how to lose weight, and meetings in a city-owned building. Somehow Nidetch was made aware of it. There, facing her fears and the hard-ass approach they fostered, broaching no sympathy and no real emotional support, she lost twenty pounds. The Obesity Clinic insisted on a loss of seventy-four pounds, which Nidetch knew she could not accomplish unless she surrounded herself with like-minded souls who were on the same path. She called a bunch of her friends who had weight problems, and they shared their hidden cookie feasts, the chocolate cravings, the sneaked meals between the meals, of mostly wheat, flour, and sugar. They referred to their food slips as "Frankensteins." Out of the original forty members who met at her home, Nidetch created what became known to the world as Weight Watchers.

How did she know that she needed a support group? It was not the time yet of women's consciousness-raising groups to which many of us later belonged in the late sixties. I joined a group like this, not focusing on weight but on women's empowerment, with Marlo Thomas, Gloria Steinem, Flo Kennedy, Suzanne Levine, and others. This was 1968, seven years after Nidetch had her brainstorm about needing a support group to solve her food problems. Like Bill Wilson and Dr. Bob Smith, who had founded a program for alcoholics in the 1930s, Nidetch somehow understood that she could not do this thing alone.

She drew together a group of women friends who were in the same overweight boat. She put together a food plan using some of what the Obesity Clinic was advocating, plus other items she had discovered in the preceding years of diets and diet doctors. One of the things that Nidetch insisted on was that her friends have doctor's appointments to assess their health before starting on the food plan that she was suggesting. This requirement continues to be part of the Weight Watchers program even today. Nidetch viewed compulsive eating as an emotional problem and wanted to treat it with an "emotional" program. Because she was not a trained nutritionist, she did not want to take the responsibility of suggesting a food plan and urged clients to find their own doctors to prescribe healthy food plans.

Like many of us, Nidetch knew the score about food. She knew about proteins and vegetables and exercise and knew what foods were good for weight loss and what were not, having proved her theories on herself for decades. But also, as they did for many of us, these diets and the knowledge of what worked still resulted in gaining back the weight. Early Weight Watchers, with its group idea, was a new one for weight loss. Most of Nidetch's male contemporaries would avoid the mention of "groups" of dieters and focus on the lone dieter, with his or her food, a book (that the doctor had probably written), and his or her own conscience.

Of course, if conscience could do the trick, most overeaters would not have needed anything else.

In a short time, forty women were gathering each week in Nidetch's home for meetings about their weight problems, and Nidetch had lost the seventy-four pounds she originally intended to lose. Opening up first her home and then rented meeting sites, she soon had thousands of men and women enlisted in her program. Weight Watchers was incorporated with the help of a couple who had been clients and had lost weight through the program. Al Lippert and his wife, Felice, helped the Nidetches market their new company.

By 1968, Weight Watchers was a public company and a household name. Meetings were cropping up all over the country, and soon in Canada and Europe. With her flair for public speaking and her strong and positive program, Nidetch was reaching millions around the world through appearances on *Good Morning America, The Tonight Show, The Merv Griffin Show,* and others. Weight Watchers, Inc., was worth $28 million in 1978. Later the company was sold to Heinz; by 1998 it had grown to a net worth of $42 million. (Today, Oprah Winfrey has a 10 percent stake in Weight Watchers.) There were at least twenty-five million Weight Watchers members in twenty-nine countries by the year 2000. My friend Judith Goldman reminds me that Weight Watchers is sort of a bridge between the Anonymous programs and severe diets.

In my experience, anyone who has had a remotely serious problem with weight has tried Weight Watchers at least once, and many people still swear by it. Not me, unfortunately. While the world welcomed another new program, I would remain aloof and fighting my demons, still thinking I could handle this thing by myself.

CHAPTER 12

MY JOURNEY

My Entrance into America's Folk Music Revival

I used to be Snow White, but I drifted.

—MAE WEST

By the end of the summer of 1962 I knew I was physically ill. When I drew in a breath, my lungs were gurgling as though a waterfall was plummeting down my rib cage into my chest. Did it interfere with my singing? I didn't think so, and if it was not interfering with my ability to make a living, I ignored it.

I had a big break in the middle of an emotional turmoil that autumn. I was invited to open for Theo Bikel at Carnegie Hall. I was overjoyed. My mother and father came to New York from Colorado to see my debut, and all of Peter's extended family showed up (his sister-in-law's family owned Bergdorf Goodman and threw me an after-concert party on the top floor of the store). The concert was a wonderful success, but I was on the edge of a precipice, caught between my husband and my lover—and my terror. By the time the party was in full swing I was a mess, and afterward Peter and I had a shouting and shoving match at the hotel. His brother Gary, whom Peter had told of my affair, threatened to make sure I didn't get custody of Clark if Peter and I divorced. Two days later, in Tucson, where I had my next club appearance, I had to be hospitalized when the gurgling waterfall in my chest was diagnosed as tuberculosis.

I was finally stopped in my madness, in my tracks, in my dash for the door, in my perpetual motion. I insisted that before I was admitted to the hospital my friends drive me to a liquor store where I bought a six-pack of beer and a huge bottle of Kahlúa, one of my favorite sweet drinks at the time. Sugar AND alcohol. Then I was shut down, hospitalized, first in Arizona at Tucson General Hospital for a month, during which I went through my booze stash in no time. My friends from the club kept the Kahlúa and beer coming. The doctors did not approve, but they didn't take it away.

I spent the time healing, writing letters to my husband telling him I wanted out of the marriage, writing to Clark to tell him I loved him and would see him soon, writing in my journals of my confused and unhappy thoughts, and writing Albert Grossman that no, I did not want to join a trio of women he was bent on calling the Brown-Eyed Girls. He had put Peter, Paul and Mary together, telling me that I was the fallback choice if Mary hadn't worked out. Albert saw how I was struggling and didn't think I could make it on my own, hence the trio idea. It was to be me, Judy Henske, and Jo Mapes. He told me he would get me brown contacts, his idea of a joke—Henske had brown eyes and Mapes and I would have to get brown contacts. I had agreed hastily—after all, he had made Peter, Paul and Mary into an international franchise. Now I changed my yes to a no. I would go it on my own, no matter what. I was going to do it my way or die trying.

I never thought I was going to die in the glorious Arizona desert, where the light and the color on the mountains I saw from my screened-in corner room were inspiring and healing, from golden sunrise to watercolor sunset. I was there, in the peace and tranquillity, receiving healing drugs for my illness, for a month. Then I was off to National Jewish Hospital in Denver for another four months of drugs and rehab, thanks to Theodore Bikel who was on the board at the hospital and put in a good word for a struggling, sick singer who had no money.

Peter had brought Clark to Denver to be with me, and my son was staying at Mom's so I would be able to see him every day. She would pick me up and take me home to my old house. Peter was sure our marriage, once I began to heal, would be all right. I knew it wouldn't, but was grateful that he had brought Clark to Denver. I would practice the piano for an hour or so, play with my son, and drink a couple of Manhattans, my mother's drink of the moment. Then she would drive me back to the hospital for the night, where I would have a slimming dinner of steak or chicken or fish, and smoke a lot of cigarettes. I had no appetite at all, so I ceased worrying about food and smoked like a fiend. It seemed that everyone smoked at National Jewish Hospital.

Years after Peter and I had parted we slowly became, I think, reconciled to each other's gifts and defects. We were both, in our own ways, working on our careers and the hard-won things that those careers would require—our separation and the freedom to go our own ways. I wish that those had not been the terms of our faltering marriage, but that was the truth, and the truth, it was said, could set us free. Or at least set me free.

In January, after he went back to Connecticut, Peter arranged for Clark to be spirited out of Colorado (I called it kidnapping, which is what it was) under cover of darkness and secrecy, as we had no formal separation agreement or pending divorce agreement. I was, of course, devastated and called the local attorney general in Colorado for help, but he informed me that Peter was the father and could do what he wished, with or without my consent.

As I recovered in the safe environment of National Jewish Hospital, with my guitar and my notebooks, planning my next album (when have I not been working on my next album?), I had my first facial from a woman named Ava, an immigrant from Israel who had been sent to the mountains of Colorado to recover from TB. Her gift set a standard for self-care that has lasted me well into my seventies and has led to many other kinds of healthy routines that still support my emotional, physical, and spiritual life and make it possible for me to thrive as I move from one day, one month, one year to the next. I knew I had to find a way to fight my demons with good habits—exercise, massage, facials, getting my hair treated, learning more about my profession, working toward good eating and drinking habits.

When Ava administered my facial with her lovely, slender fingers and took away the tension and gave a glow to my skin, I was hooked for life on these marvelous techniques for body, mind, and spirit, and I still use them, from massage and facials to salt glows, mud packs, water massage (Thalasso), and of course exercise, which I have used for years to counter my depression.

I understood by now that I had a calling, knew that the body was the instrument, not just the voice. I also knew that I was in imminent danger from drinking and overeating. A facial, a massage, an hour of exercise, a life-giving session of Alexander bodywork, or a session at a Karnofsky physical therapy center where I swung from the trapeze rings would keep me on track. I could be sweating and screaming with delight, and I knew it would mean the difference between staying alive and healthy or dying of alcoholism or becoming too obese to work. It might not save me from choking to death in some foreign bathroom, but the good habits would have to fight against the bad habits. I hoped they would keep me alive until a miracle arrived.

In February, after a painful visit with Peter in Denver, I filed for divorce and was allowed a short leave from the hospital. I went straight to Washington, D.C., to perform on *Dinner with the President,* a celebration of John F. Kennedy. I was feeling much better but still had a few weeks more of hospitalization and drugs to take, though I had been given a green light from my doctors in Denver to travel.

At the Shoreham Hotel in D.C., I was greeted by Harold Leventhal, my manager. On the program with me were Josh White, the Clancy Brothers and Tommy Makem, Lynn Gold, Robert Preston, Will Holt, and Odetta. It was wonderful to meet JFK in the flesh—he was so excited about life, so engaging, so charming and vital. At that time, he was the great hope for peace, for enlightened government, for an end to the Vietnam War. His eyes and his smile when he shook hands with me were dazzling. It was January 31.

By the end of November he would be dead.

Being in his presence for just a little while will stay with me forever.

I flew back to Denver and the hospital, where I completed my treatment. After another two months I was released and gathered my luggage, my guitar, and my skis and wedding silver—the only things I got from Peter in our divorce. I settled in Greenwich Village, where my lover and my people were. I soon had an apartment on West Tenth and Hudson, which I shared with Vera Hertenstein, who worked at Elektra Records. There would be no more home in the hills of Connecticut for me, except trips to pick up Clark and bring him to the city. I began to rethink and revive my work life with the help of Harold Leventhal. It was a slow process and for me the most important part of it, after I was clear that there was no going back to my marriage, was getting time with my son. Visits to the court in Connecticut where Peter had filed for custody were part of the weeks and months to come.

But my drinking was getting worse as I ate what I pleased, favoring sugar, carbs, and junk, and began a descent into the deep depression that finally compelled me to get help. Walter, who had been my lover but now was mostly a friend, was seeing a therapist who seemed to be helping him with his own depression. A friend of ours, who was a singer with a drinking problem, had found therapy helpful in curbing the worst of his drinking. I had already applied to the William Alanson White Institute, but had not heard back from them. I got the name of our friend's shrink and made an appointment for the end of August, when therapists in New York traditionally return from their summer houses.

The man I went to see, Ralph Klein, was part of a

group who called themselves the Sullivanians. They followed the writings and teachings of Harry Stack Sullivan, or so they said. Their ideas about living in groups, parents sharing the raising of their children with other parents, free love, and open marriage were things that my peer group had no problems with. Ralph and I had a good and, as I see it now, rather old-fashioned therapist–patient relationship. We talked about everything. He was sensitive and intelligent, well-read, and seemed to know what he was doing. In our sessions—one hour-long and one two-hour session a week. He was always very professional, kind, and generous, even inviting me to Amagansett where he and the rest of the Sullivanian clan owned houses on the beach on Long Island. Clark often played with Ralph's son Josh, and the boys became good friends. After my first sessions with Ralph, I began to feel happier and less depressed.

Slowly I found my professional footing again, started making more records (I had two out and in 1963 made a third, and then a fourth, of my first solo concert at Town Hall, in 1964, all of them on Elektra, where I would record for the next twenty-three years). I had good times with Clark, sometimes in the city, often on trips we would take to Colorado. Peter, though the divorce settlement was slow in coming, was generous with visitation rights.

I was traveling more and more all over the world, recording albums, and having ever-increasing success, with my career gaining ground every year. With Ralph, I was able to explore my suicide attempt as well as my failed marriage and my childhood in a dysfunctional alcoholic family. I began to talk about my secrets, the fear, the terror. Even the drinking, about which I was honest. He did not feel it was as serious as I knew it was. Still, with all the traveling I did, I managed to keep an amazing number of my appointments with Ralph. My therapist was there to catch me when I fell, as well as to encourage me to fly.

I had therapy with Ralph for seven years, and with Julie Schneider, my second "Sullivanian" therapist, for another five, the years my career was zooming from nadir to zenith. By 1970, I had started to achieve a place at the top of my profession, having platinum albums and great successes. The thing none of my therapists talked about with me was my serious struggle with food. Or I should say I didn't reveal my growing problems with food, and they took the drinking as a natural outlet for my anxiety—in fact, many of them suggested to their patients that alcohol was a good thing, certainly better than pills, to deal with depression and anxiety. I was getting worse and knew it. My therapists didn't seem to take my fears to heart. I would often call Ralph, and then Julie, in the middle of the night. I would say I was afraid I was going to do myself harm and ask if they thought I should be hospitalized. They always told me to come see them in the morning.

Even with these huge holes in their knowledge about drinking, I still think the Sullivanians taught me about discipline and connecting with other people and in many ways gave me the support I needed to become a working artist. They supported my efforts to follow my dreams. They knew nothing about addictions, although most doctors did not in those days. Their reaction to my drinking was that everyone drank, and that alcohol was good for the nerves and preferable to drugs. They did not prescribe drugs—they were psychologists rather than psychiatrists.

I told my therapists I suspected I was going down. I knew the drinking could kill me and suspected that the food might. And I knew by then that I was truly an alcoholic, that I would drink to the end, drink till I died. That was the spirit! Show 'em who's in charge!

They say you can find your own enablers and I did. The Sullivanians often suggested their patients drink to soothe anxiety. I stayed with them for fifteen years.

I kept telling myself, You can control the booze, and the food, you can do this!

And even if I *were* dying, at least I would go down on my own terms.

CHAPTER 13

LIVES OF THE DIET GURUS

Donaldson, Pennington, Atkins,
Stillman, Taller

Life itself is the proper binge.

—JULIA CHILD

In the 1920s in New York, Dr. Blake F. Donaldson, a cardiologist practicing on New York's Upper East Side, noticed his heart patients were gaining weight and so was he. He was determined to find a diet that would restore their health. Donaldson knew one had to be vigilant, and that adhering to a strict diet is not everyone's cup of tea. He decided to find out what diet worked best for total heart health and created the strongest skeletal structure in humans. Advised by a fellow doctor that certain bones at the American Museum of Natural History might give him the answer, he spent long hours studying the skeletons of Greenland Inuits.

These bones had come to reside at the museum as the

result of a request by Frank Boas, an anthropologist who in 1897 had asked the Arctic explorer Admiral Robert E. Peary to bring back some Inuit tribal members from Greenland. Peary complied, inviting six Inuits to board the *Hope* for a trip back to New York, where, he assured them, they would find money, fame, and a new home. The Inuits were intrigued and excited.

The *Hope* arrived in New York Harbor, at which point Admiral Peary, feeling the Inuits would be a great attraction, invited the public to view his charges. Twenty thousand visitors made their way to the *Hope* to see the Inuits. For 25 cents a view, the crowds came to gawk at these remarkable creatures, who were clad in their native furs. The money Peary raised would be used to fund his next expedition. His captives, though they had been willing to sail with the great explorer, must have felt peculiar being stared at by strangers. They were then escorted to the museum, where they were housed in the basement as guests of the city. In the coming months, as they were studied by scientists, many of them succumbed to tuberculosis and other diseases to which they were not immune. Far from the whales, bears, and fish that constituted their diets, most of them perished. Only one child, Minik, survived. He was the son of Qisuk, who had died. William Wallace, who worked at the museum, adopted Minik. As a teenager, he convinced his adoptive father to take him back to Greenland, but he soon returned to New York, where he died of influenza.

The Inuits' remains were preserved for scientific research. In the 1970s the museum tried to return the remains of the Inuits to their Greenland relatives who refused to accept them. Not only were they superstitious about the ancestral ghosts that might still haunt their countrymen's remains, but they had no ceremony for burial in their culture.

In the mid 1920s, Donaldson consulted Vilhjalmur Stefansson, an explorer who had spent a lifetime studying the Inuit, even living with them for five years. Stefansson had lived on the "biologically perfect foods" that the natives ate—such as fresh whale meat—and found these to be the perfect diet. Other explorers, including Shackleton, Scott, and even Peary himself, agreed that these were the best foods, and that the people in these regions who drank water and ate mostly red meat, and few if any vegetables, had perfect health. Donaldson used mainly these foods in his diet for major weight loss in the first months for his obese and overweight patients.

Donaldson's suggested diet consisted of one porterhouse steak (six ounces of meat, two ounces of fat) three times a day—if you want more of the protein, feel free—and half a cup of black, sugarless coffee.

Compared to the way I eat today (generous, satisfying, delicious meals), this looks like a prison diet—that is, a first-class prison with porterhouse steaks available three times a day. And Donaldson insisted this was it. You lost the weight, and after you have reached goal weight, add one new food a day: potatoes, peas, grapefruit. If you regained the weight, you went straight back to the porterhouse steak diet once again.

Many were inspired by Donaldson's rigorously daring plan, which certainly worked for a lot of people, at least those who could be "rigorous," but it was pretty hard-core. After all, the Inuit in Greenland and Alaska had lives that were very different from yours and mine. Weight would probably not have been a concern.

In 1958, a good twenty years after Donaldson's foray into the red-meat diet, Dr. Alfred W. Pennington published "A New Concept in the Treatment of Obesity" in *The Journal of the American Medical Association*. In the article, he promoted the concept of eliminating all sugar, flour, grains, and carbs and increasing fat and protein in the diet. Pennington had been hired by the medical division of the DuPont Company and was asked to find out why the usual diets were not working on its employees. He developed the concept he called "eat fat and get thin," and the DuPont employees did just that, in enough numbers to convince Pennington that his approach worked. It was more forgiving than the Donaldson plan, and very effective—at least for a while.

Pennington's original diet, which he published in 1953 in the paper "Treatment of Obesity with Calorically Unrestricted Diets," was simple. It included walking at least half an hour a day, as well as a daily routine of exactly eight hours of sleep a night. He recommended going to bed at the same time every night and never sleeping a minute more than eight hours. On the Pennington diet, you are encouraged to eat three big meals a day and lose seven pounds of excess weight a month. And each of the three meals has two courses: Course One is six or more ounces of any red meat, with fat but no salt whatsoever. No salty meats or dishes either—that is, no bacon, smoked ham, canned chicken, frankfurters, canned or spiced meat, or salted beef. Course Two is a "regular helping" of potatoes, sweet potatoes, boiled rice, grapefruit, melon, banana, pear, or berries.

Now the question: What is a "regular helping" of anything? I never had a clue.

On Pennington's plan you may also have water only—six glasses a day and a whole lemon in the water of one of those glasses. No bread, flour, salt, sugar, alcohol, or anything else not mentioned. Many plans are the same today, but may include salt and diet soda, as well as black tea or coffee. Pennington gave the employees at DuPont this food plan and it was so successful that he started treating patients outside of DuPont with the diet and began writing books.

Through the early decades of the twentieth century there were many tantalizing plans for losing those few extra, ugly, annoying pounds, or even that hundred pounds you had to get rid of. There was the Liquid Diet and the Spring Cleaning Diet. There was the Basic Seven Diet, the Famous Clinic Diet, the Hard and Fast Diet, and the Daily Dozen Diet. There was also the disagreeably titled Fat Girls' Diet (sent to you by mail in a plain wrapper at special prices). Under the aegis of the Fat Girls' Diet there were the special diets for fat stomachs and thick waistlines, the How to Stay Thin After Fifty Diet, the Special Diet for Fat Hips and Thighs, the Dehydration Diet, which was "for girls who crave sweets." And on and on ad nauseam. Literally.

In the early sixties, we come to Dr. Robert Atkins. The publishing business, television, and a growing market of people who wanted to lose weight and lose it fast found Atkins and his accessible and popular books quickly. Unlike some of his predecessors, his publications were not hidden in obscure journals but were trumpeted to the world of dieters, runners, and fast-moving people who wanted what Atkins had—a solution! The William Banting of the mid-century American diet had arrived.

Atkins was born on October 17, 1930, in Columbus, Ohio. He grew up in Dayton and sold shoes for a while and worked at his father's restaurants. He had a spot on a radio show in Dayton, then went to the University of Michigan, contemplated a career as a stand-up comedian after graduation, and worked at resorts in the Adirondacks before going on to get his medical degree in cardiology at Cornell University Medical College (now Weill Cornell). He graduated in 1955 and opened a practice of cardiology and complementary medicine in New York.

In the early years of his practice, Atkins's weight crept

up to 225 pounds and he couldn't lose it. The Pennington approach worked. Atkins certainly understood the power of protein since it had worked on his own body and weight loss, and I suspect Atkins was aware that certain specialists feared that too much red meat might cause heart attacks, a popular idea then and today, yet he began to suggest Pennington's ideas to his cardiac patients. As a consultant to AT&T, he then helped his own group of overweight patients reach their ideal weight. He began to modify the plan, put his stamp on the exact nature of the food and the plan itself, and launched his own high-protein, low-carb diet.

I was fast to get on board. My actual dieting, above and beyond the cutting out of cream, sugar, desserts, and bread, consisted of eating as little as possible, not eating all day till the evening, having only protein and vegetables, and never giving up booze. Atkins was a wonderful discovery for a while, as long as I was able to sustain it.

In 1965 Atkins went on *The Tonight Show* to promote his new nutrition plan, which was soon all the rage. By then it included the famous ketone sticks, on which you would pee and hope to see purple, indicating your body was using stored fat instead of what you were eating (which for me was mostly beef and cheese).

At the time I was touring all over the country and the world, and the Atkins diet worked for me. Lots of protein, beef, eggs, and cheese, but no wheat. And no junk.

I did lose ten pounds soon after I started the diet. I did not lose it quickly because I would not give up alcohol. I knew I had to have the booze to feed the beast.

For a short time, Atkins was a lifesaving approach for me, like most of the diets I went on. And then I gained the weight back.

And I was smoking like a fiend.

Vogue published the Atkins diet in 1970, furthering the rush to use his mostly protein approach. He published *Dr. Atkins' Diet Revolution* in 1972. Atkins was not only a diet guru but a popular celebrity, maybe the first since Gaylord Hauser. I followed much of the Atkins approach for those years, combining it with other things I found, including a trip to a doctor who gave me a series of colored pills that included uppers and downers—speed and opiates—that I took happily, and lost more weight in the bargain.

In the late sixties, I found Dr. Max Stillman's diet. Born in 1896, Stillman was a family doctor who worked in Brooklyn and would treat more than ten thousand overweight patients during his medical career. His approach was also high protein, low fat, but the Stillman diet had some very important twists, which included the promise that you could lose twenty-eight pounds in thirty days and still have buttermilk, steak, and booze. This approach thrilled me. I could drink and lose weight, and it was legal.

Stillman was famous for saying that by raising the "fires

of metabolism" using protein as 90 percent of the diet, the fat can be "melted out of" the body's storage facilities. He franchised his approach, and between 1967 and 1974 published *The Doctor's Quick Weight Loss Diet*, *The Doctor's Quick Inches-Off Diet*, *The Doctor's Quick Teenage Diet*, and *Dr. Stillman's 14-day Shape-Up Program*.

I switched onto the Stillman diet at once, as did Karen Carpenter, whose extreme dieting and the kind of strident fasting I was fond of was something I totally identified with. Her indulgence in the methods I was using would lead her into anorexia and death. A food addict, as I know, can overdo anything and become sick on plans that might be healthy and successful for others. It is not the fault of the diets themselves, which work perfectly, until they don't.

Stillman died in 1975, at a normal weight. Karen died of heart failure in February 1983 from her eating disorder. I stayed with the Stillman diet on and off, until I was drinking so much that I couldn't keep track of anything.

Dr. Herman Taller was another pioneer in the field of dieting. A Romanian-born obstetrician and gynecologist, he had a weight problem (who of our heroes so far has not, dear reader, had a weight problem?) that he was determined to solve. As he studied all the diets he encountered, he decided that "there is no longer any question that obesity is a disease . . . and a grave one." As he ballooned to 265 pounds on a frame of five feet ten inches, his doctor first put him on an unsaturated fat regimen, and Taller began losing weight. He understood that carbohydrates had been his downfall, and realized he needed to develop a balance between "fat formation and fat disposal," which he found could be achieved by eating more protein and adding the fat from the protein, as well as oils from nuts, fish, and other sources. Then he came across Pennington's theories in a medical journal in 1951 and read: "Contrary to the claims of the low-calorie school of thought, low-calorie diets have failed . . . There are fat people, plenty of them, who are actually starving." And, "The ability of tissues to oxidize fat, in contrast to carbohydrates, is unlimited." When Taller began to include fats—krill oil among them—and Pennington's idea of fat burning fat, his weight plummeted.

As Taller researched further, he found the William Banting (our hero!) pamphlet from 1846 and began to understand that to burn fat one's body needed fat—not starch, not sugar, not grains, not flour. Polyunsaturated fat, the oily "mystery" substance in those days, was helping Taller's body eliminate the unwanted pounds. Nuts, seeds, fish, algae, and krill are sources of these fats. Even at five thousand calories a day, on this regimen of high protein, low carbohydrates, and oils, he lost sixty-five pounds in eight months. He realized the low-calorie diets were killing people with kindness and allowing them to be deceived in their search for the right weight-loss program. *Calories Don't Count,* published in 1961, would put a damper on the 1,200-calorie rule of intake.

Taller's book suggested:

1. Three full meals a day
2. Never leave the table hungry if you want to stay slim
3. Eat large portions of beef, meat, fish, or fowl
4. Include in your meals pot roast, fried chicken, cheesecake, and mayonnaise

Taller's theories about high protein and polyunsaturated fats were strongly condemned in 1962 by George Larrick, the commissioner of the Food and Drug Administration, who said that the prescribing of safflower oil capsules for the treatment of obesity (a product that was recommended by Taller, who had an interest in the company) was worse than worthless. Simon and Schuster, who published *Calories Don't Count,* refuted the FDA's charges, saying their vicious attack had no bearing in reality. The same old story from the FDA, which is constantly trying to belittle, besmirch, and downplay attempts to find alternatives to medical treatments that rely on drugs manufactured by pharmaceutical companies, whose products are boldly pushed in doctors' offices by salespeople from these self-interested companies. (The FDA is also lobbied by drug companies.)

Taller's popularity defied the criticism and his book wound up selling two million copies. One can still find copies, not in pristine "just published" condition but certainly in good shape. His plan obviously worked, at least for some and at least for a while. Today one of his biggest favorites, and also one of the bestsellers in diet marketing, is krill oil, a good source of the polyunsaturated fats that Taller was advising, along with food plans free of sugar, wheat, grain, and flour. Krill are red shellfish, tiny and plentiful, living in every ocean in the world. Unlike fish oils, krill oil contains no mercury. Krill oil is said to protect against heart attack, improve vision and memory, relieve joint inflammation, slow the aging process, lower cholesterol, improve emotional stability, clear up acne, and improve the immune system.

What's not to like?

CHAPTER 14

MY JOURNEY

The Heart of the Matter

> Man is the only animal that can remain on friendly terms
> with the victims he intends to eat until he eats them.
>
> —SAMUEL BUTLER

In 1965 I was still under my top weight of 140, and to
some people might have appeared to be thin. I had (and
still have, even on my best days) what is called body dys-
morphia disorder, and I was always convinced I was fat.
In many of the photographs from the mid-sixties I appear
to be normal, certainly not bulging at the seams, but my
mind told me something different. By this time I was
using speed and downers, prescribed for two weeks at a
time, the most I could get from my doctor. They were
keeping my weight where I wanted it to be, around 115,
and increasing my addiction to pills and food as well as
alcohol. And I yo-yoed, losing and gaining ten to fifteen

pounds in spite of often carefully eating very little, never a whole meal, never anything with fat, no butter, no oil, no dairy, always feeling deprived, dieting, exercising, fasting, watching my calories, and making myself crazy with fad diets. Meanwhile, my touring and recording career was growing stronger every year.

At the same time the question of custody of my son continued unresolved. I wanted and needed, for Clark's peace of mind and my own, to have custody verified in court. The hearing at which the judge would finally determine the outcome of years of pleas and lawyers was constantly being put off for one reason or another. Years were overwhelmed by this conflict as I waited for an answer from our lawyers who promised me "the mother never loses." I tried to be hopeful, but there was an undertow of sadness I could not hide.

For three years I had been sharing a one-bedroom apartment in Greenwich Village with Vera Hertenstein. Our little apartment was near the Gaslight, the Kettle of Fish, Gerde's Folk City, and Washington Square and was the perfect place to be a part of the "folk music revival."

But I needed more space for Clark, especially after the social worker from the court in Connecticut came to assess my living situation, smirking at the small space, the traffic on West Hudson, and Greenwich Village in general. I located an apartment on the Upper West Side at 164 West Seventy-ninth. It was a few blocks from my therapist. I had my furniture and meager belongings shipped up from West Tenth and settled in. The rent was only a hundred dollars more than it had been in the Village, and I bought a fine Steinway grand that sat in the center of the largest of my otherwise bare eight rooms, filling my head with dreams of getting back to practicing Mozart and Rachmaninoff. Now I had space for my son, for my friends, and for my family when they came to visit. Now Richard and Mimi Fariña and Malvina Reynolds and her husband, Bud (who left an electric can opener as a house gift), could come for a few days. Phil Ochs, Eric Anderson, Steve Katz, and other musicians sometimes needed a place to crash, and now there was room at my place. It would prove to be a lucky address, as have been all three of my homes in the Big Apple.

For a year I had been losing my voice every few weeks, since I was touring and traveling and having to sing most every night. I had never really studied singing, but I knew I was not going to be able to continue my career if I did not solve the vocal problems. I asked Harry Belafonte's guitarist, Ray Bogaslav, who he thought I should study with. He told me there was only one person he would recommend: Max Margulis. I also asked my friends Irma and Mordecai Bauman, who ran Indian Hill, a well-known arts camp in the Berkshires. It was popular with many successful musicians, dancers, and singers, Arlo Guthrie and Carly Simon among them. The Baumans gave me the same name: Max Margulis. Max had taught Laurence Olivier to sing for his role in *The Entertainer* and had many fine European singers as students. I had no idea whether Max would want to teach me and had put off calling him, but my voice was hoarse and I was worried about not being able to sing. Now that I had moved, it was time to make the call.

I still had Max's phone number, but no one seemed to know his address. When I called he was polite but seemed reluctant. He asked me what kind of a singer I was, and when I told him he said he really did not want to teach someone like me. He said people who sang what I sang were not serious. I begged some more, and he reluctantly said we could meet, that I should come by that afternoon. I asked him where he lived and said I would be right over.

I walked out my front door, apartment 8A, turned right, went past the elevator, and rang the bell to 8C. Max answered the door and asked me how I had arrived so quickly. When I told him I lived next door he smiled and said he understood now that it was meant to be. We began our lessons.

Max wanted me to come for lessons every day and often I would. His wife, Helen, would greet me with a cup of tea and we would talk to her parakeet, Papagano, while I drank the tea and refused the cake she always offered. The walls of their apartment were full of the paintings of Max's friends—Willem de Kooning and Arshile Gorky. I basked in the care of a true genius of the voice.

The technique Max taught was primarily bel canto,

an approach that focuses on the clarity of the vowel and freedom of phrasing. I started out with barely an octave to my voice. I had been able to sing clearly when I was young and for a few years when I started recording. Now, worn out and vocally tired, I would have to warm up for half an hour before I could warble a melody.

Max and I worked diligently as he helped me to bridge the gap between my upper and lower registers. Within a year or so my vocal range, instead of being limited to a few notes, became one long and uninterrupted line of three octaves, which had been waiting in the wings all along. I studied with Max for thirty-two years. It took every one of those to get where I am today. There have been setbacks, of course, both physical and emotional. My drinking and my eating disorder got in the way of my progress, but still I knew that I was on the right track with Max, and I somehow also knew I was going to need all he had to teach me so I could sing comfortably for as many years as I would need to. He never let me down.

At the time I discovered Max and was also preparing to perform in the Soviet Union, I found out that my three-year court fight to get custody of Clark had ended with a decision against me. Peter was granted sole custody. I was devastated and tried to cancel everything, including my upcoming trip to Poland and Moscow, feeling I was too jarred, too depressed, and too fearful of doing harm to myself. I needed someone who could comfort me and keep me steady.

Fourteen years younger than I and five years older than my son, my sister, Holly Ann, was eleven and mature for her age. We had always been very close and she was like my own child in a way. My mother agreed that she could travel with me, and she made the trip emotionally and physically possible for me. She was a shining, bright spirit on that remarkable journey.

Eating in Poland and Russia was a challenge. Part of the problem was that I could never get enough booze and was probably detoxing at times. Our Polish host and translator was very generous with reading all the menus that included many pastries stuffed with delicious ground meat and there were lots of beautiful sweets, which I indulged in without reservation. I was shy about asking for more vodka, even then a favorite of mine. Polish vodka, some of it anyway, is very dark and rich, and I managed to hide a quart of it in my luggage when we flew to Moscow. Our Russian translator, we later realized, told us only about the meals she liked on the various menus, and we ate well and heavily. Again I found it difficult to order the amount of alcohol I really needed to self-medicate for my depression. I gained a few pounds in spite of restricting, which I was doing a lot of anyway, partly due to the sorrow I was feeling. I was looking forward to seeing my son at the end of the summer, but was heartbroken that we would not have a chance to settle in to what I had hoped would be our home in New York.

When Holly and I returned with amazing memories of a trip that turned out to be very special to both of us, we reunited with Clark for the rest of the summer of 1965 in a rented house on Long Island, before I took Clark back out to his father in Vancouver, sad but knowing I had no choice. (Peter meanwhile had moved to Vancouver to teach at the University of British Columbia.) He would start school and I would see him every vacation, and every summer, and every time I could wrangle visits through my ex-husband.

In the years that followed my loss of custody, the rock and the roll of the folk music revival, with me as part of its epicenter, rolled on. There was work to do, concerts and albums to arrange, and a life full of music, which saved my sanity and gave me the opportunity to travel and to see Clark often.

But the stress and the food and the drinking were bearing down on me. I never missed a show; I was always working and always running—as I did as a child—from pillar to post, as my mother would say. I was busy fighting the demons all day, every day. Thoughts of suicide plagued me when I was eating, and despair would follow my outings to the store, where I would buy the things I loved to binge on—Mars bars, doughnuts, marzipan, Rice Krispies cookies (like my mother used to make), divinity, and fudge. Anything chocolate, I was not particular. If I could not find dark chocolate I would settle for milk chocolate. A feast was not enough and a famine was what I longed for.

I could not keep the pounds off and could not *not* drink.

But I fought like crazy all the time to do things differently. Among other problems, my clothes presented a challenge. I had to get into them, and I was starting to feel the pinch and wanted to look the way I had looked, say, a year before. I used the pills that were prescribed by my doctors and did the restricting on a daily basis—no this, no that—but then, suddenly, I'd eat everything in the cupboard! In addition I was continuing my addiction to exercise (what is now referred to as exercise bulimia), and it kept me fit and hid my insanity. When I see pictures of me during those years—one with my foot planted on a chair at the Newport Folk Festival, singing harmony with Leonard Cohen—I know by the look of my bare leg, thin and sleek in my sandals, that I had been using those magical pills!

I fasted during those years and made many attempts to be thin and ethereal, and I tried many drugs, including LSD and an occasional magic mushroom. They all made me paranoid, and they all made me hungry.

During the sixties there was a great search for nirvana and peace of mind through meditation and flower power, and I sampled the cuisine and the hallucinogens that often went with those quests. Mostly I drank, but occasionally I would smoke some dope. It once took two bottles of Jim Beam to bring me down from an LSD trip I took with John and Michelle Phillips. LSD didn't help, and my trip on acid was so bad I did it twice! But I was still hungry when I landed back on earth. Hungry and scared I was losing my mind.

No more psychedelics for me! I would drink, and although I knew I was an alcoholic and talked about it to a dozen therapists, I never tried to stop. If I were truly an alcoholic, I would make every effort to live up to my birthright, my inherited gift of genetics. There was the promise of success in those genes, and I believed, in spite of the emotional turmoil, drinking, and food obsession, that I could succeed. And I did. Year after year I ran my business, did the work I had to do, learned new songs, recorded albums, played concerts, and plunged ahead with determination, overcoming the booze, the food, the despair, the mental turmoil.

At least I thought that was what I was doing. I was fighting against the odds and I thought I was winning. Sometimes I even believed I was succeeding. Therapy helped me and the therapists I saw enabled me to drink. There was great support for all I was doing, and the drinking got ignored, as well as the eating.

My father was still alive and would be for another two years. He was selling insurance, as the radio career had stalled out after television came to Denver. He was in despair about his life. His depression was peaking and he talked to me about it. I told him he had to get into therapy and found a therapist for him in Denver.

My mom had jobs at Blue Cross and Neustater's, a fancy dress shop in Denver. My siblings, whom I adore, were growing up. Mike, four years younger than I, was at Denver University getting his doctorate; David was in the marines; and Denver John was at Mount Hermon, a private boarding school in the East. Holly was still home, but soon would go to High Mowing in New Hampshire, a Waldorf School where she would begin her pursuits as a weaver and painter.

Even though I was not able to see Clark as much as before, we still had wonderful visits when we could a few times a year. But missing my son, wishing I could see him more, was always with me. Perhaps part of that sorrow drove my drinking and my eating disorder. But everyone has reasons for sorrow.

It was a fiery time, a time of great music, wonderful collaborations with other singers, writers, and producers. There were many great, unknown artists to discover, and I helped to give some of them exposure, and to make their songs famous as well. From Randy Newman's "I Think It's Going to Rain Today," to Joni Mitchell's "Both Sides, Now," to Leonard Cohen's "Suzanne" and "Sisters of Mercy," to Richard and Mimi Fariña's "Pack Up Your Sorrows" and "Hard Lovin' Loser," from Eric Anderson and Tom Paxton to the Beatles, I recorded songs I loved and was out on the road, performing in the United States, Australia, Japan, the U.K., and sometimes Europe, and then settling down for wonderful times with Clark in New York, Vancouver, and Colorado. In the reunions with Clark, my mother, my father, and my four siblings, there were joyous times amid my sadness when my son asked me why he could not live with me in New York.

By 1967, I had started a new phase in my career when I began to write my own songs. My demons appeared in a more useful light while I was sitting at the piano and focused on the words and the music. I began to rediscover some of the peace that had always come to me when I was a child, practicing the piano, learning pieces, memorizing Chopin and Rachmaninoff. As I wrote those first songs of many to come over the next decades, I was also becoming stronger as a performer as Max taught me how to sing. I began to have a consistency and a vocal range I had never known. Max assured me that I would be able to sing anywhere, anytime, at the level I was coming to depend on. I started to believe it.

The miracle finally occurred at the end of 1967. My ex-husband called to say that after thinking it over he had come to the conclusion that Clark would be better off living with me.

To say I was overjoyed would be putting it mildly! I met Clark at Kennedy Airport the next day and went immediately to get the papers for my custody. The first thing he told me was that he wanted to grow his hair long. I was happy in all the ways that counted, and hoped Clark's arrival would heal my heart, which it did.

But not my alcoholism, and not my eating disorder.

They would have to wait.

CHAPTER 15

LIVES OF THE DIET GURUS

Dr. Andrew Weil

We lose our health—and create profitable diseases and dependencies—by failing to see the direct connections between living and eating . . .

—ANDREW WEIL

In our panoply of diet doctors, none is more cutting-edge, innovative, and old-fashioned in some ways while modern in others than Dr. Andrew Weil. This remarkable physician has chosen the road less traveled in his searching, clear-eyed assessment of the various opportunities and choices we can make for our own health. In his investigation of diet, alternative medicine, body work, vitamin therapy, and the use of both traditional (homeopathic) and Western (allopathic) medicine, he shows us a new path into the sunlight of healing, a new vista of possibilities.

Weil has famously written that "sugar, starch, refined carbohydrates, and trans-fats are more dangerous to the human body than saturated fats." We know this; we have heard this mantra over and over from the diet gurus. Here is a practitioner of the holistic approach, telling us more about this new, fresh alternative.

Weil also has succinct words about the treatment of depression: "The best way to treat depression is to exercise strenuously seven times a week for thirty minutes and eat a lot of broccoli." He suggests that the solution to obesity is to eat less food and exercise more. Weil also uses ancient practices and has an old-school attitude about hands-on health care with the fresh idea that we must be our own health advocates.

Weil is the director of the Center for Integrative Medicine of the College of Medicine, University of Arizona, which he founded in 1994 and where he practices a combination of alternative and conventional healing arts. A client can find acupuncture, herbal remedies, classes in meditation, vitamin D and omega-3 fatty acids therapy, and many other treatments. He suggests that if a patient is already on a conventional, prescribed medication, they stay on that therapy and incorporate the nonconventional treatments slowly, thereby enhancing the body's ability to fight illness, infection, and addiction.

Weil was born in Philadelphia on June 8, 1942, the same year that a Japanese submarine was found in the mouth of the Columbia River; the Battle of Midway ended the war in the Pacific; the Disney film *Bambi* was released; and Paul McCartney, Elaine "Spanky" McFarlane, and Graham Nash were born. And I was three years old.

Weil was an only child. His parents were secular Jews and his father was a milliner. His parents worked together in their shop, and often young Andrew would spend time alone. He could amuse himself in the yard around his home, a place of flowering and—probably to Andrew—magical beauty. Perhaps the guided imagery and the self-hypnosis Weil discovered in his work as a healer began in that small yard where time and attention and love are strong components of gardening. He would later come to believe that the mind can and does heal the body. (Think of the *decision* to make a change as just as important as the actions taken to achieve that change.)

Weil has said that for him, religion was always "gardening, the care and growing of living, essential things from mother earth." He also got a kick out of the giggles of his grandmother Mayme, who, when she'd had a few drinks, began to laugh uncontrollably. Her little grandson would become somewhat hysterical over her mood and, he, too, would laugh. Perhaps the experience made him conscious of the physical action of the body changing the mood of the moment. Like the Indian yogi Sai Baba, who recommends laughing for fifteen minutes upon arising to dissipate depression, Weil later would advise people to use what he called "laughing yoga" to heal their dark moods.

In 1959, when Weil was seventeen, he was awarded a scholarship from the American Association for the United Nations, an organization started by Eleanor Roosevelt to educate and inform people around the world about the United Nations. He traveled to Greece, India, and Thailand and has said that his interest in non-Western medical treatments began on this trip. The knowledge that there are many paths to healing would follow Weil through his career.

Returning to the States, Weil entered Harvard in 1960, where he would eventually earn a degree in biology and his medical degree. At Harvard he was also introduced to the lectures by Timothy Leary, a psychologist, writer, and proponent of the positive effects of hallucinogens, and to his assistant, Richard Alpert, later known as Ram Dass, the author of *Be Here Now,* which was about his experiences with hallucinogens. Leary and Alpert were researchers and teachers at the Harvard Psilocybin Project and also started a private group known as the Harvard Psychedelic Club, in which participants explored the world of psychedelic drugs—LSD, psilocybin, magic mushrooms, and other hallucinogens. Like many people in the sixties, Weil read Aldous Huxley's *The Doors of Perception,* in which the author describes his experiments with mescaline, meditation, and what he called "sacramental vision." In its review of Don Lattin's *The Harvard Psychedelic Club: How Timothy Leary, Ram Dass, Huston Smith, and Andrew Weil Killed the Fifties and Ushered in a New Age for America,*

The New York Times said: "There were late nights, new drugs, unhinged libidos. A version of the 1960s was being invented, one dazzling trip at a time."

Allen Ginsberg, Alan Watts, and William Burroughs began to tune in, turn on, and show up. It was the early sixties, and it was rumored that even JFK was introduced to LSD in those heady days.

The Center for Research in Personality, over which Leary and Alpert presided, was managed on a very high level as Harvard's center for the exploration of LSD, psilocybin, and other hallucinogens. These drugs were legal at the time, but the very nature of the party atmosphere that surrounded the research presented unforeseen problems.

Eventually Weil would become a staff writer for *The Harvard Crimson*. In 1962 Robert E. Smith, an editor at the magazine, broke the first story about the methods that were being used by Leary and Alpert in their research in psychedelics. He knew people who were involved with the groups, and some who were unhappy with the way in which the research was being handled. His article exposed the controversy that was beginning to disrupt their research.

Leary and Alpert claimed their research was scientific and that they were meeting all the requirements of their contracts with the university, one of which was that they not include undergraduates in their research. But the party atmosphere was getting out of hand and making many people in the administration and the student body nervous. There were rumors of younger people with mental and emotional problems who had bad experiences under the guidance of the two gurus of drug-induced bliss.

Weil began having misgivings about Leary and Alpert's research methods. The research into hallucinogenic use was becoming a "scene," instead of what was originally intended as a research project.

On May 28, 1963, *The Harvard Crimson* published an article titled "Corporation Fires Richard Alpert for Giving Undergraduates Drugs!" Joseph M. Russin and Andrew Weil cowrote the piece, stating that Harvard's president, Nathan Pusey, had fired Alpert because he and his group at the Psychedelic Club were giving mind-altering drugs to undergraduates. The article said this violated the agreement Alpert had with the university. Leary was also in the process of leaving the university at about this time, under a rather indeterminate cloud—perhaps sensing more criticism coming down the road and that the project was soon coming to an end.

The article by Russin and Weil was a sort of "roundup" of the history of the research methods that had backfired as well as the scandal around Leary, Alpert, and the club. The actions had already been taken, the damage already done when the article appeared. Weil might have been a canary in the mine, but he was certainly not the only one singing.

Leary and Alpert were gone from their teaching positions, though Harvard was to continue research on hallucinogenic drugs. Hurt feelings and many questions survived, though each of these men—as brilliant and in disagreement as they were—went on to success in his own way.

After the tempest in the Harvard psychedelic teapot, Leary became the Johnny Appleseed of the psychedelic new age, Alpert became Ram Dass, and Weil, combining all the best of what he was learning, became a true teacher and powerful advocate of complementary medicine, and a man who understands much about healing.

After receiving his doctorate, Weil moved to San Francisco for an internship at Mount Zion Hospital in 1968 and volunteered at the Haight-Ashbury Free Clinic, amid the whirl of hippies of the Jefferson Airplane generation. It was certainly a high time, full of young people who wanted to change the world. Weil *would* change the world.

He says he made a conscious decision not to practice the kind of medicine he had been taught at Harvard. In *Spontaneous Healing* he wrote that "I came to realize, early in my hospital days, that if you rely on such measures as the main strategy for treating illness . . . you expose patients to risk, because, by their nature, pharmaceutical weapons are strong and toxic. Their desired effects are too often offset by side effects, by toxicity."

In 1972 Weil published *The Natural Mind,* his first of many books. He has been ahead of the curve in weight loss and overall health for decades, ahead of most of his

Western medical peers. Early on, before many understood the body, mind, spirit approach to health, Weil discovered and recommended practices that would become part of the repertoire of many health professionals. I have always been impressed by any medical doctor who speaks of natural and alternative healing as the road to total physical and mental health, and Weil gave hope to compulsive eaters and people with alcoholism and weight problems. He recommends exercise, diet, acupuncture, and homeopathic methods as a matter of course, in a time when most people still do not consider them essential for mental as well as physical health.

In *Spontaneous Healing,* Weil says: "Doctors believe that health requires outside intervention of one sort or another, while proponents of natural hygiene maintain that health results from living in harmony with natural law." Weil was also onto a solution for compulsive eaters: get rid of sugar, grains, and wheat. In an interview with Larry King, Weil described his practice as the curing of the "visible unhealthy state of the body in which the person and the misery lives."

Weil has also been an advocate for the healing art of bodywork; he has studied and often uses in his practice Rolfing, Alexander bodywork, tai chi, craniosacral therapy, reflexology, massage, and spiritual paths to healing. All are often appropriate for whole-body health, posture, flexibility, and reduction of tension.

Weil has brought many of us out of the dark ages. We

have more balance now and can go to a massage therapist or a homeopathic practitioner instead of the ER, or go to the Center for Integrative Medicine. There are many choices for treatment if you have an eating disorder. Weil, like all the other diet gurus, is adding more dimensions to our search for mental and physical health.

Sugar, grains, flour, wheat: those are the killer foods, and now we can move toward spiritual, emotional, and physical health to keep them from killing us.

CHAPTER 16

MY JOURNEY

The Late Sixties and the Seventies

You must be the change you wish to see in the world.

—GANDHI

It was 1968. Clark was nine years old and living in New York with me. He had new friends and a new school (the Professional Children's School). We had great times; we cruised around Manhattan Island on the Circle Line, went to the theater, and had playdates with his new friends from school and from our building. He wanted drums and we got them from the renowned Manny's Music store. There were excursions to the American Museum of Natural History. I got a potting wheel and a kiln and put them in what had been our dining room, and we both learned to wedge clay and try to stop the pots from falling over, screaming with laughter when they did. I hired a wonderful housekeeper, Dahlia, who took care of us and made us beans and rice, Clark's favorite meal, and I read stories to him at bedtime and sang to him during the day. It was a wonderful time. His hair grew out, he smiled all the time, gained a few inches every week, it seemed, and was happy and glad to be with me. He talked to his dad once a week, which I oversaw, to make sure he did not lose touch.

But I did not realize my son was a budding addict, or that there would be many years of pain in his life because of his genetic pool, which included what was also killing me slowly.

I was literally getting sicker, having what by now was a full-blown eating disorder. I was agonizing over every meal with every diet I could find. I was still in therapy, as I had been since 1963. My workouts were pretty extreme, and because I was smoking, I could hardly breathe. I was eating and drinking up a storm as well.

My drinking was by now taking up much of my attention and my attempts to find out why I had to drink so much were as unending as the attempts to find the right diet. The depression I had always suffered from came in and out of my life. I treated it with exercise, continuing on the compulsive workouts (I had to work out no matter how tired I was—biking till the sweat poured off my face, jumping up and down on my hardwood floors till my feet ached, bending and stretching till I felt my face glow with sweat).

My father died in 1968 of an aneurysm. The day he

died I was in London, where I was playing a concert at Royal Albert Hall. My brother Denver John was there, having taken off time from school to travel with me. My four siblings and I were always close, Denver John and I extremely so, and it was my brother who took the call and brought the news to me. We flew straight home for the funeral, lost in sorrow and Jack Daniel's.

I had written a song for Daddy, "My Father," three weeks before his death. He had been such an influence, such a powerful force, and of course an alcoholic like I was. I was heartbroken that he had suffered as he had, this blind, handsome, wonderfully talented man who had inspired me, and who died depressed and in some ways beaten, and who had lived a life that his blindness might have smothered in someone less determined, less talented, less remarkable. I swore I would win the ground for him that he had somehow missed in the fight. I did not even understand that it was sobriety I was struggling toward.

In June I went to Los Angeles to make my seventh album for Elektra. The day I arrived Robert Kennedy was killed. I was holed up in a rented house on Mulholland Drive. Clark and I settled into the many rooms, the swimming pool, and the sorrowful days that followed the murder of another Kennedy. I longed to cancel the recording session and take my boy home to New York, but we had to move ahead and get the job done. I had to make music to heal and help heal those around me.

My producer David Anderle planned a surprise for me. He brought in the renowned guitar players Buddy Emmons and James Burton from Nashville; Chris Ethridge, the bass player with the Flying Burrito Brothers who would later spend many years with Willie Nelson; Van Dyke Parks, a brilliant arranger and writer for California groups like the Beach Boys; Jim Gordon, an acclaimed drummer whose cocaine addiction would later drive him to murder his mother. And after we got started learning the songs at the studio, in walked Stephen Stills, lately of Buffalo Springfield. My eyes opened wide.

When Stephen added his guitar to the mix, the whole place lit up. I couldn't believe his playing, and his energy and dynamic ability put the right touch on every song and made me sing better than I ever had. They say love is a matter of chemistry, and the chemistry in that studio, with the rugs on the wooden walls, the sound of that incredible band, and the presence of this handsome guy, was a magic elixir that transcended everything—sorrow, anxiety, loss, and pain. Our tumultuous affair began, I think, at once. It did not last long, but before it was over I had cut ties with many people, including Michael Thomas, the wonderful Australian I had been living with for two years in New York. On a trip home, I said I was in love with another man, and Michael, wise as he always was and always is, bowed out. It was a passionate, intense, feverish, bicoastal romance that proceeded to unfold with Stephen. I was swept off my feet, but in a few months the intense rush was too much for me and before it had really begun, I withdrew. The passion was there in the song Stephen wrote for me, "Suite: Judy Blue Eyes," and in the pain I think we both felt long after the fire had burned out. The song did more than stay with me, it stayed with the world, and every time I hear it I am overcome with feelings for all the things we had lost, not just a romance. I was fighting a battle with my drinking that drew everything good and happy with it. I ran, which was what I always did, away from the romance, into my own dark place where no one could follow me, not even Stephen. I ran back to my therapists. (There were two things Stephen made clear that he hated—New York and therapy—and I was in both.)

Stephen and I had a rapturous love affair during the making of *Who Knows Where the Time Goes*. But nothing ever stopped my eating, my drinking. Stephen was into his own emotional struggle while starting Crosby, Stills and Nash, closing out Buffalo Springfield. It couldn't have been easy, and I drank enough for both of us. When the dust had settled and I had returned from Los Angeles to my home and my cats in New York, the affair was over.

I got a call from Joe Papp in March 1969 asking if I was interested in being in a musical at the Public Theater's Shakespeare in the Park. I said I was not. The new album was doing well and I had a lot of concert dates that summer. Joe was persistent and finally I said I would listen to the songs that John Morris (who usually wrote scores for Mel Brooks) had written for an adaptation of *Peer Gynt*. Joe wanted me to meet with the director. I agreed after finding that I liked John's songs and that I would be acting with Stacy Keach. I decided I needed a summer break from touring. It would mean more time with Clark and being in one place for three months. It was, as the kids say, a no-brainer.

When we had our first rehearsals in May, I met Stacy, who was starring in the lead role as Peer Gynt the wanderer, a metaphor not only for him but for me. Handsome and articulate, by then becoming well known in his field, Stacy was a very powerful force in the theater and soon in my life. I did not expect anything but a summer of nights in the Delacorte Theater and days with Clark. The drama of my romance with Stephen had left me longing to be a part of something exciting again. Stacy had that excitement, and before I knew it my head was spinning and I was in love.

My eating disorder was always all over the place. I dieted, lost a few pounds, went on a fast, lost more weight, and then went back to the pills for a few weeks. During the next four years with Stacy I knew I was drinking myself to death, and couldn't stop. And I was fighting my weight every day.

In 1969, I was starting my way down to the bottom of my drinking and my eating disorder. Blackouts were a regular part of my days and nights. I could still hold off drinking until after the show, but I drank every day. Most people would have thought me a happy woman. But I was possessed with the need to eat and drink in excess, always on a diet and compulsive as ever about exercise. I was in love, but I was miserable and had nightmares and anxiety attacks as well as blackouts and days where I was as out of it as a high-functioning addict could be.

Most obese people I have known do not eat in public. They hide food, as I hid food; they eat in solitude and, like me, might have very simple meals with friends and family. They talk of avoiding sugar, how they have lost a few pounds, are going to the gym. We wish to be relieved from the sorrow and desperation that sugar and wheat bring to every meal, the depression, hopelessness, and suicidal thoughts, and the fuel for therapy, the fuel for sadness. Most of us would do anything to get rid of the fat. At times I came close to killing myself with my food obsession. You don't have to eat too much to die from this disease. You can eat too little as well. And the wrong things.

I have been there, just not obese, because I was always either restricting, throwing up, exercising to the max—and most of the time, all three. I once belonged to three health clubs in New York—the Paris, near my home; the Park on Fifty-Seventh because it was open twenty-four hours a day; and one of the new swanky steam, sauna, and pool clubs next to Saks. I stocked a locker in each club with comb, shampoo, swimming suit, body cream, and anything else I might need. I was often drunk when I arrived, and once ran into a wall at the Paris, sending blood running down my face. When a fellow swimmer pointed it out to me, I was not at all shocked when I looked in the mirror. I needed to detox and I needed to swim, and I needed to keep my weight down, and I would do anything to make that happen. What was a little blood?

Taking diet pills (speed) to stay thin, adhering to any and every diet there was, hiding food, I was just as sick as the person who carries the weight around. I might be thin, but we have the same illness.

Every waking moment was spent trying to get into my tiny size 2 or 4 pants and keep my weight under 120, or under 115 or 110. I did not realize I was crazy, my mind fighting constantly for control of this illness that I did not know was an illness. I thought I could manage both the food and the booze, but they would bend me until I nearly broke.

I would arrive in Colorado for a visit and my mother would have prepared one of her divine meals with all the trimmings. I would be on one of my "not this, not that, not any of these" diets and would poke my fork at a piece of rare steak and a leaf of lettuce and she would say, "I just don't know what to give you to eat anymore." Her voice would be full of sadness. It breaks my heart now to think of it. Today I would eat the moon to please her if it would bring her back.

I lived like that for years, close to the edge, clinging to my sanity, on the knife edge of my dangerous path. I was still smoking and gaining weight no matter what diet or what fasting program, or what pills I was taking.

In 1969 I started classes at Elizabeth Arden's elegant salon on Fifth Avenue, where twice a week I donned a pink leotard and worked out, sweating with Arden's exercise guru, Miss Craig. She got me toned and touching my toes, bending everything in my body that would bend. She was enthusiastic and professional, and when I told her I was going to be on the road and would not be able to come to her sessions as much as I had in the beginning, she encouraged me to keep up the good work.

The Royal Canadian Air Force exercises were a short and sweet method of keeping in shape. I used it when I could not get to Miss Craig. The program was developed in the late fifties by Bill Orban for the overall fitness of pilots in the Royal Canadian Air Force, many of whom were thought by their superior officers not to be in proper shape to perform their duties. The exercises, which were tailored for use by people who were going to be in situations where they could not get to a gym, had to be fast and to the point. When I found this series of exercises in 1970, I knew they were meant for me. But because I was still smoking, even these simple exercises, which took about ten minutes, were extremely difficult, even after having been to see Miss Craig on a regular basis. After a few weeks off the road, I decided I had to stop smoking to be able to breathe again.

In the spring of 1971, Stacy was filming *Fat City* in Stockton, California. It was directed by John Huston, and the cast included Stacy as the lead, Jeff Bridges, Susan Tyrrell, and Candy Clark. It was the story of some down-and-out prizefighters who end up badly, a real tearjerker, with the fights played out in real time, on and off the screen. I was in a knock-down, drag-out fight of my own, so it was a powerful counterpoint to my struggle.

I decided to take a break from New York. That January, after we had experimented with a couple of schools in New York, Clark, Stacy, and I had found a private school in Maryland for Clark. He was doing well and his recently developed habit of using drugs seemed to have been curtailed. No one knew in those years that Clark was, even at his young age, in need of rehab. No one would have thought it then.

I left my shrinks for a few weeks and took a hiatus from concerts and recording. Stacy and I rented a house with a pool by one of the canals in Stockton. I swam every day, trying to work on my weight. I was attempting to quit smoking and cut down to three cigarillos a day, but it was a losing battle. My eating disorder was driving me crazy. I began to stuff food into my mouth, as if I had been let out of a cage. All bets were off, all diets down the drain, neither the little blue and pink pills nor the most recent Atkins diet and all-protein food plans were working. I began to pack on the pounds. All the control I had been able to muster in the years preceding Stockton went out the window.

One night Stacy and I had a big dinner party for the cast and crew at our house. I was a pretty good cook in those days and had made Indian curries—three kinds, I could never stop at one: fish, chicken, and vegetarian. I spent the morning shopping, preparing, cooking. The whole house was scented with cumin, coriander, curry, onions, and bubbling sauces. There were bowls of chutney and white rice with the kernels separate and perfectly cooked, the way I liked it. There was a huge salad from a local garden with my famous oil, vinegar, mustard, garlic, and salt and pepper dressing. I was starving, as usual, having eaten nothing all day, waiting for the great dinner and the great desserts I had made—fresh fruit pies for the amateurs and chocolate fudge for the serious sugar addicts like myself.

Everyone working on the movie came over, swimming and sunning in our pool, splashing and shouting, enjoying their day off and the warmth of the California sun, then hungrily waiting for dinner. As the afternoon wore on and the sun faded, everyone drifted into the living room for more drinks—whiskey for John and Stacy, beer and wine for the actors and crew. I was drinking vodka, as usual. While I ran around the room, putting out chips and guacamole and pouring drinks, the crew talked of other days, other films they had worked on together, reminiscing about the previous glories they had shared.

Dinner was served, and I ate more than all the hefty guys in the living room. I remember standing in front of the mirror in our pink bathroom, with the gold handles on the sink and the sweet-smelling soaps that were like flowers in their dishes, looking at my puffy face. In the gilded mirror, I peered into my eyes, reaching for another little cigar, and suddenly the thought came into my head that I could simply bend over the toilet, put my finger down my throat, and get rid of the entire meal. It was the solution to all my problems! I reentered the party, happy, brilliant (or so I thought), quite drunk, and knowing I had discovered something wonderful that would take away the pain, at least for that moment, that day, that night.

And so another layer of terror was laid onto my life, and I began living in what was deeper addictive wreckage. As I let go of smoking, reluctantly having the cigarettes and the cigars pulled from my fingers by what felt like a force greater than myself, I was also becoming an active bulimic, skilled at the practice, depending on it, reveling in it—until, of course, it turned on me. For eleven years, I would be purging almost every day. I didn't know what I had was called bulimia. I thought I had invented it. News of the athletes who used bulimia to keep their weight down was news I never got, or I probably would have started throwing up much earlier. It was a nightmare. I was at one of the high points of my career, but the devil had found me where I lived and was going to keep coming at me until the despair threatened to drive me to complete the act I had rehearsed at fourteen.

I was thirty-one, and my eating disorder was taking over my life and everything natural was shutting down, including my period—resulting in the osteoporosis that I now have to deal with—while I ate and threw up and wept in remorse. Sometimes I still took those little rainbow pills that had been prescribed by one of my many doctors in New York. They kept my appetite down while I sped all day and passed out at night after drinking too much.

I was truly a working addict, a type A, nothing seemed to stop me, and the discipline I had learned as a child only reinforced these traits. Looking at me you might not know I was suffering from addictions. My career continued to flourish and I accomplished many things—my life blossomed and my fame spread. I had top-ten records, traveled all over the world, sang at Carnegie Hall and Royal Albert Hall. And my life was falling apart.

In 1975, the movie I had made about my teacher, *Antonia: A Portrait of the Woman,* was nominated for an Academy Award, received the Christopher Award, was shown on PBS a number of times, and opened in a limited theatrical run. Mike Wallace interviewed Antonia Brico on *60 Minutes.*

Brico's story had haunted me since the days when I had

studied with her and played with her orchestra. I wanted people to know this story of a woman who became the first female in musical history to conduct major symphonies. She was a pioneer, and I put my own money into producing it and codirected with Jill Godmilow.

Antonia Brico was born in Holland in 1904 to an unwed mother and spirited to America when she was three by her foster parents, where she had grown up in San Francisco. Clearly musical at an early age, she then studied piano at Berkeley where she had been possessed by the outlandish idea that she could become a conductor.

There were no conductors who were women at that time. Everyone told Brico she could never conduct orchestras; no one would hire a woman. She had defied them all and gone on to study conducting and graduate from the finest conducting school in Germany. In 1929, the year she graduated, she conducted the Berlin Philharmonic, the greatest orchestra in the world at the time. The reviews were ecstatic, many saying the male conductors who were the pride of Germany at the time had much to learn from this slip of a girl at the head of the magnificent symphony.

Fresh from Berlin, she debuted with the San Francisco Symphony to more magnificent reviews and went on to the Hollywood Bowl and worldwide tours with the Sibelius Orchestra, the London Symphony, and other great orchestras. She had conducted and managed her own orchestra at Carnegie Hall during World War II and had already had an illustrious career when she landed in Denver, having been told she would be offered the podium of the Denver Symphony. On her arrival in Colorado, with her Steinway pianos; statues of Beethoven, Mozart, and Bach; and all her worldly goods, expecting to begin her job conducting the symphony, the board of directors decided Brico could not be elected to the position of maestro because she was a woman. Had they not noticed before? They said she would not be able to join the Cactus Club—a well-known club frequented by the elite gentlemen of Denver, whose pockets were lined with gold and who might give money to the orchestra— so she would not be able to do the most important job of a conductor, which is raising money.

With the nomination of *Antonia*, Brico's career was launched again. The success of *Antonia* helped her get back to conducting major symphonies, and she was written about and interviewed and celebrated. I don't think she ever forgave me for leaving my Rachmaninoff concerto and turning to folk music when I was a teenager, but she and I had remained friends and now she had her career back. It was a gratifying experience when Jill, my codirector, and I took her to Hollywood for the Academy Awards.

Successes were also happening to me in other areas, and I had Grammy nominations and gold and platinum albums. I made records for Elektra records, usually one every eighteen months and sometimes one a year; I studied and worked, practicing and enlarging my professional skills. All the while, I was getting sicker and sicker every day. I thought throwing up was the answer to all my problems.

I did not know then that death is the last binge on the block.

CHAPTER 17

LIVES OF THE DIET GURUS

Linus Pauling, Adelle Davis, and the Vitamin Revolution

Max Margulis was the first person I heard talk about Linus Pauling, a scientist, humanitarian, and recipient of the Nobel Prize in Chemistry in 1954 and the Nobel Peace Prize in 1962. Pauling was considered the most internationally important scientist since Antoine Lavoisier, the Frenchman who founded the field of chemistry in the eighteenth century. Pauling was also one of the first scientists to discover the healing powers of vitamin C, for which many in his field called him a crackpot. Today, the value of vitamin C is known, and people use it regularly to protect against colds, flus, and other illnesses.

Pauling became an advocate for the use of vitamin C and other minerals in the maintenance of physical as well as mental health. In 1970, in *Vitamin C and the Common Cold,* he proposed that physical ailments as well as mental abnormalities might be successfully treated by "correcting imbalances or deficiencies among naturally occurring biochemical constituents of the brain, notably vitamins and other micronutrients, as an alternative to the administration of potent synthetic psychoactive drugs." He was on the cusp of the alternative medicine flood of the late sixties and early seventies. Popular books in which Linus Pauling detailed his nutritional recommendations, like *Cancer and Vitamin C* (with Ewan Cameron) and *How to Live Longer and Feel Better,* set off a backlash from the scientific field in which he had previously gained renown. By the time he was into his heyday of natural health remedies, the drug companies had begun the infuriating fight against anything that would deter their profits and diminish the godlike status of doctors. Pauling was in their direct line of fire.

Born in Portland, Oregon, in February 1901, Pauling was educated at Oregon Agricultural College (now Oregon State University) and got his postgraduate and doctorate degrees in chemistry at Caltech, where he studied atoms and how they bond with magnetism to form unique structures between molecules and crystals. He started teaching at Caltech in 1927, where he pursued intensive research, which led him to investigate the new field of quantum mechanics. He received a Guggenheim Fellowship to continue these studies in Europe, and when he returned to Caltech as the head of freshman chemistry, he published his findings in his first book, *General Chemistry,* in which he proposed new theories based on the chemical bond approach—the basis of current research on human genomes. Pauling began his studies in human health in the late 1930s around the time Adelle Davis's book *Optimum Health*—the first of her books about nutrition and vitamin therapy—was published. Pauling was awarded a Rockefeller Foundation Grant during that decade to work on the molecular structure of proteins. This research would lead him, in later years, to study the value of vitamins and minerals in the support of human health.

During World War II, Pauling invented a meter for monitoring oxygen levels for incubator babies and surgery patients, developed synthetic blood plasma (used in emergency battlefield clinics), and discovered the alpha-helix, the basis of the field of molecular biology. In the aftermath of Hiroshima and Nagasaki, he became an outspoken advocate for the control of nuclear testing and a spokesperson for abolishing nuclear war. In today's world, his concerns are the concerns of anyone who works in the field of nuclear armaments, anyone who is a human living on this dangerous planet where nuclear warheads dot the landscape of many countries. His work as a proponent for peace garnered him the Nobel Prize in 1962 as well as the Gandhi Peace Prize, the Lenin Prize, the Albert Schweitzer Peace Medal, and numerous honorary doctoral degrees from universities and colleges around the world. Many universities in the United States have created their own Pauling lectureships and medals to honor other scientists.

Pauling had always encouraged scientists to be involved in politics and society, saying, "One way in which scientists work is by observing the world, making note of phenomena, and analyzing them." In 1964, after forty-two years at Caltech, Pauling was forced to leave his tenured post because of his political activities. The Nuclear Test Ban Treaty that he had fought six years for was finally signed in 1963 by the United States, Great Britain, and the Soviet Union.

It was a time of great political upheaval in the United States. I was in the midst of it too, singing at antiwar protests and working against the Vietnam War. My fellow performers and I were often blacklisted from television and concerts, and the feeling in the country was that there were two sides, and the side you were on could determine whether or not you got or kept a job. Pauling was, in effect, fired.

In spite of the outcries of his contemporary scientists and their anti-naturalist publications, like *The New York Times* and the *Herald Tribune,* Pauling was much sought after as a speaker for conferences, political rallies, commencements, and media programs. He also became a professor emeritus at Stanford and established the Linus Pauling Institute of Science and Medicine for research and education, following his belief that nutrition could prevent, ameliorate, and/or cure many diseases, and "slow the aging process, and alleviate suffering."

Vitamin C was proven in many research experiments to be helpful in promoting a "regimen for better health" and as the keystone to the relief of many ailments and to the support of ongoing health.

Pauling died at his ranch near Big Sur in 1994. He was ninety-three. That day the world lost a great humanitarian as well as a great scientist and promoter of physical, mental, and emotional health. His ideas permeated all levels of the population, from the most sophisticated scientists to people who spend their lives working to promote peace.

Adelle Davis was also called a crackpot during the course of her career as a nutritionist. Born in February 1904 in Liston, Indiana, she was educated at Purdue University and the University of California, Berkeley. She received a master's degree in biochemistry from the University of Southern California Medical School. She then moved to New York where she was trained in diatetics at Bellevue and Fordham Hospitals and was soon consulting with obstetricians about nutrition. Davis was an advocate for vitamin therapy and unprocessed food and spoke about the dangers of pesticide residues and additives in our food chain. Americans became avid followers. She was a rebel, speaking out against the big companies that created food that was unhealthy, full of fat, sugar, salt, and added corn. Her views about vitamins urged us to use them, and I listened to her advice, beginning my long and winding vitamin and nutritionist search, which I strongly feel has added to my health and my ability to ward off illnesses, even as I was going down with an eating disorder.

When I was in Lenox Hill Hospital in New York in 1966, being treated for hepatitis and mononucleosis, a friend brought me Davis's book *Let's Get Well*. When I first read her books, they made me think about vitamins and diet and what might have caused my hepatitis. She said diet was the cause of illness, and I believed her. I started taking the array of vitamins she recommended, including C and multivitamins, as well as vitamin B complex, which probably helped me recover from hepatitis, as well as helping my immune system ward off many other things I might have gotten but did not! *The New York Times* referred to Davis as an "oracle," and she was compared to Ralph Nader. She was a frequent guest on *The Tonight Show*, where I heard her talk about her ideas. I agreed with *Life* magazine, which referred to her as the "High Priestess" of food.

In the midst of my growing eating disorder, *Let's Get Well* was on my kitchen counter. Davis took up a lot of air in the world of diet and health, and garnered a lot of criticism, as well as suits for damages resulting from her ideas about minerals and health. She also wrote a book about her experiences with LSD called *Exploring Inner Space,* which she published under the pseudonym of Jane Dunlap. Though at the time she was called a quack, today many of her theories about vitamins have gained credibility. Vitamins A and D have been proven to have healing powers and are considered to have beneficial effects on many ailments. (Vitamin D for bones is now trumping bisphosphonates with many doctors, along with ipriflavone, vitamin K, and the natural steroid DHEA.) Davis was ahead of her time in many ways.

But many of the suggestions she made about the use of vitamins and minerals tended to be loose in their dosage and application, and in some cases there were few proven studies to back up her assertions. Davis was often quoted as saying that she never saw anyone who drank a quart of milk a day or who ate bacon, as she did, get cancer. She stopped saying that when she was diagnosed with cancer in 1974, but still she left behind a legacy of ten million books sold and, according to Stephen Barrett, M.D., "a following that was large, devoted, and misinformed." This criticism was a sign of those earlier decades, when scientists thought they had all the answers and derided nutritional approaches, or what we now call "alternative."

Davis was fond of saying that "the balance of the right vitamins in the diet can maintain and even cure illness."

Davis became one of the best-known, as well as one of the most reviled, diet gurus of the century, in part due to her incomplete research. But she was on to the problems that were emerging in the business of food production, and the dangers of additives, sugar, corn, and pesticide residue. Patrick Leahy, our wonderful senator from Vermont, supported Davis's ideas, saying, "Now the weight of medical evidence—including former Surgeon General Koop's Report on Nutrition and Health—has vindicated her views."

Acupuncture and homeopathic remedies have stood me in good stead in getting rid of my asthma and the accompanying lung and allergy symptoms that plagued me for years (and interfered with my singing), and I completely support alternative medicine.

Also, as my homeopathic practitioner says, "If you use all of these alternative remedies and still feel awful, go to a hospital!"

Though she died of a cancer she was sure she would never get, Davis was a healer and one of the people who first guided us to take a look at how our food is processed, our need for vitamins, and the consequences of sugar and junk in our diets.

TOP: Clark Collin Taylor, 1989, St. Paul Minnesota.

MIDDLE: Collin, our great-grandson, with a sly look on his face as he prepares to launch that snowball at his Papa Louis. Vail, Colorado, 2016.

BOTTOM: With my beautiful grand-daughter, Hollis Taylor, 2016.

TOP: Calling my agent in my wedding dress, 1996.

MIDDLE: With my mother, Marjorie, at my wedding at the Cathedral of Saint John the Divine, New York, 1996. When Louis Nelson and I were married, we had been together for eighteen years.

BOTTOM: In my white hat, with my beautiful Persian kitty, Coco Chanel, queen of fashion and feline style.

TOP: In my living room in New York, 2004, sitting on my antique couch with an angel. I'm wearing something beaded and thinking of the next album.

BOTTOM: With my beloved son, Clark, in New York, 1968. Linda McCartney took us to Riverside Park, where we cleared off the snow and spent a few hours with Linda talking and watching our breath freeze in the air while she took our pictures.

TOP: With Joan Baez at the Newport Folk Festival in Rhode Island, 2009. We sang *Diamonds and Rust* together.

BOTTOM: With Leonard Cohen as he was being inducted into the Songwriters Hall of Fame, 2010, in New York.

TOP: With my sister, Holly Ann, in the mountains outside of Cody, Wyoming, 1991.

MIDDLE: On the set of a television program, Los Angeles in the late sixties.

BOTTOM: Cooling off in the dress from the *Wildflowers* shoot, 1968. I was photographed by Jim Frawley somewhere out near Topanga Canyon.

TOP, LEFT: Mother's day, 2016, while recording an interview for PBS that appeared on *A Love Letter to Stephen Sondheim* with the Greeley Symphony at the Boettcher Auditorium in Denver.

TOP, RIGHT: With Louis at Natalie Collins's wedding in New York.

BOTTOM: Rehearsing in 2011 for my PBS pledge drive concert at the Temple of Dendur in the Metropolitan Museum of Art in New York.

TOP: Ari Hest, the singer-songwriter with whom I wrote and recorded duets for the *Silver Skies Blue* album in 2016. The collaboration with this amazing young artist was a first for me.

MIDDLE: In concert at the Gilded Garter, Central City, Colorado, 1959.

BOTTOM: My handsome husband, Louis Nelson.

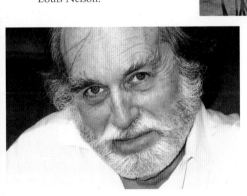

My brothers, Michael, David, and Denver John with the polar bear at the Explorers Club in New York. They were all dressed up for the wedding of our niece, Natalie.

In Vietnam in 1996, when I was a UNICEF Spokesperson for the Arts. I visited schools, hospitals, and communities on behalf of the UN and spent time with these gracious, beautiful people.

CHAPTER 18

MY JOURNEY

Almost Nearing the Last Gasp

You have to leave the city of your comfort and go into the wilderness of your intuition. What you'll discover will be wonderful. What you'll discover is yourself.

—ALAN ALDA

Stacy and I had a tumultuous affair, full of drama, passion, and the pitfalls of two professional people who were friends as well as lovers. I longed for a simple life, but the last seven years of my drinking were the very opposite and the very worst. They found me drunk most days as well as bingeing and purging, and I was terrified of committing to anything but food, booze, and therapists, who were truly unable to help me. It became clear that Stacy and I were not going to be the happily-ever-after couple we were during the first blush of our romance.

I was inspired in many ways by my love affair with Stacy,

and in the first couple of years I took some big risks and was relatively happy even as my drinking and my eating disorder increased their pressure on my life. During the autumn after our affair began, I recorded another album, *Whales and Nightingales,* on which I included "Amazing Grace" and other songs of a spiritual nature. I began the work on *Antonia: A Portrait of the Woman* in 1972, and was excited by the process of learning about a different kind of creative enterprise. My energy surged, as did my songwriting, even as I was going downhill physically, mentally, emotionally, and spiritually. It was going to be a long descent, but who would question a person who was, on the outside, so successful at carrying on?

Near the end of my fourth year with Stacy, I began an affair with Coulter Watt, the brilliant cameraman who had filmed *Antonia.* Coulter was quite a bit younger than I was and our affair ended because I was ragged from my addictions. Now I began to realize that everything in my life fell apart and disintegrated because of them. It had less to do with falling out of love and more to do with my total inability to have continuity with anything but my career.

Another love affair, while Rome burned, found me with Jerry Oster, a reporter for the New York *Daily News,* whom I met when he reviewed *Antonia.* Jerry was clever, athletic, and smart. It lasted until he walked out on me (literally, and with very good reason).

During this time, Clark was bouncing from one private school to another and finding little peace. He had nearly died from an accident at his private school in Maryland, when he was sledding and ran into a parked car. There was a terrifying two weeks in the hospital in Hagerstown where he hovered between life and death after brain surgery. What followed were more weeks in the hospital for therapy and rehab in New York and then another school entirely, in New Hampshire, where he wound up dealing drugs.

A few weeks into the first semester at yet another school, Clark experienced a drug overdose. The school, which was in Massachusetts, was one he and I had chosen in part because the headmaster told us they took a great interest in seeing their students did not get into drugs—a promise that vanished in the wail of police sirens and, once again, near death.

Drug addiction and alcoholism have little response to a change of environment, unless, of course, one is lucky enough to get into rehab. That was going to have to wait for Clark. It was a dance of addiction and near misses, and I prayed he would live through adolescence and get well. Of course, I was still deep into my own addictions. I, too, was still some years from rehab. The dark place began to descend on me now, with no light in sight, until the beginning of 1977 when working became nearly impossible and my whole life—including relationships with friends, lovers, strangers, and concert promoters—began to go down the toilet, if you will forgive the image.

By some miracle, in 1977 Clark turned a corner. He got clean and was living with me in New York, taking the subway to St. Ann's School in Brooklyn. He turned eighteen that spring. He was the same handsome, brilliant, charming, beloved boy he had always been, but now sober. He took in my downward progression with all the sorrow of a son who sees his mother disappearing in a cloud of alcohol and depression. One morning, he looked at me across the breakfast table, staring purposely at my coffee cup. He and I both knew what was in it.

"Do you know what time it is, Mom?" he asked.

It was seven in the morning and my coffee cup was full of vodka. I just gulped down the rest of my morning medicine, knowing the cases of half-gallon bottles of vodka I had stashed in my closet would last me through the coming week, and I was glad for it.

I finished off a huge breakfast and had a couple of binges and purges that day, boxes of carbohydrates, just enough to keep me crazy—a normal day. But things were coming to a head with my drinking and my eating disorder, and it would soon not be only my son and myself who knew I was in trouble.

In 1976 I had started having vocal problems, dropping notes, getting hoarse again, and though I was seeing Dr. Weismann, my ear, nose, and throat doctor, and had been having allergy shots for the postnasal drip that was causing the hoarseness, it was only getting worse. During the spring of 1977, I would go on the road with fifteen people, including a pianist, guitarist, drummer, keyboard player, bass player, sound man, and road manager. We had long tours scheduled with many concerts, as my career was experiencing another lift, with "Send in the Clowns" on the *Billboard* chart in the top ten and a new collection of songs from the first fifteen years of my career put out by Elektra, with an album-cover photograph by Richard Avedon. That summer I started out with twenty-five concerts scheduled in as many states, and I would sing all right for the show but then not be able to the next day. Relatives and friends began calling my mother in shock.

"She has lost it, Marjorie," Aunt Jeanette would say to my mother, in tears. "Judy can't sing anymore!"

I remember one awful set of shows in the northwest. I did a concert in Portland, Oregon, after which I lost my voice. I went to the hospital to get a prescription for prednisone and saw the local ear, nose, and throat doctor. He spent a long time looking down my throat and then groaned.

"This is bad, you cannot sing on these vocal cords." His hand was shaking. It can't be easy to tell a singer she is in trouble. I said I had weeks of concerts in front of me and a huge number of salaries to pay. "We will do the best we can, but you must rest for a few days, see if we can get it back."

I holed up with all fifteen members of my band and entourage at a local motel, where the days and the canceled dates in the northwest went by, and we waited, while

I took the little white pills (prednisone), keeping silent, not talking for days on end, writing notes to people, having messages sent to New York to my lawyer, my assistant, my agent, waiting to see if I could sing. I swam in the pool, drank straight vodka, ate and purged, and swam some more. I was effectively in a daze of alcohol and food. I should have checked myself into rehab at once, but in a few days the voice would come back and I would do another concert and then my voice would blow up again.

Finally, after canceling the rest of the tour and paying off the band, I went home to New York to curl up in my bed. I was in agony. It was all going up in smoke, and there was nothing I thought I could do about it.

Jim Henson wanted me to be on *The Muppet Show,* which he was filming in London, in May. I had to call him and say I was sick, which I was, but I was also terribly hoarse. I could not bring myself to tell him that I was totally losing my voice.

"Let's reschedule for October," he said, kind and loving as usual. I had done many episodes on *Sesame Street* with his wonderful Muppets, and he was a friend. We rescheduled for October and I went on that summer, performing shows, canceling many, drinking, weeping, eating and throwing up, bingeing and fasting, and convinced I was dying.

I kept seeing Dr. Weismann, hoping the problem with my voice would vanish like magic, and occasionally there would be some improvement. Still, I had to wade through more months of concerts that were far enough apart that I might have a chance of getting through them and resting for a few weeks—weeks of more silence, more drinking, more purging, more nightmares. For the first time in my career, I was drinking not only at night but before the shows, and then during the shows. My road manager would pass me a glass of vodka before I went on, whereas in previous years it had always been after the show. I sang for the first time in blackouts now, not well and not happily, bingeing with food and drinking like a fish while my career was on a tumble to the bottom and I, who was feeling no pain, knew I was dying and could do nothing about it.

At the end of that summer, after more cancellations and some shows that were all right, I went again to see Dr. Weismann, who finally had discovered what the problem was. He told me I had what is called a hemangioma, that is, a capillary on one of my vocal cords that, like the capillaries on the face of a drunk, become engorged with blood. After more cancellations and more despair, sadness, and fear about my chances of continuing as a singer, Weismann said, "I think I have something that could work. It is new, and very few doctors have used it, because there is not much history on it. It is a laser procedure wherein the hemangioma is literally burned off the cord and should leave only a tiny scar that does not interfere with the clarity of the vocal tone. It might possibly do the trick."

I asked him what the chances were.

"Well, if you don't do it, you will continue to get worse, and your singing career will be over. On the other hand, this could work. It is your choice. I strongly suggest that you take the risk, and we have a chance that you can sing again. If we don't try this you will eventually not be able to sing, no matter how many little white pills you take."

I said I would have the surgery, and we set the appointment for October, as soon as I returned from filming *The Muppet Show*.

I was terrified, thinking every day I might not ever sing again. But I had to go on; I had no choice. To prepare for *The Muppet Show*, I went on a two-week silence before leaving for London, saving every breath for the show.

I checked into the Westbury Hotel in London, had a massage at Elizabeth Arden, slept for twelve hours straight, and went out the next day to Shepherd's Bush where Lord Lew Grade and Henson met me with champagne, a lobster lunch, and a big dressing room. They left me with hugs and kisses for good luck, and shaking in my pretty shoes, afraid I was going to blow it, I put on my costume for the taping. I was dosed to the teeth with prednisone and terrified I was not going to make it through.

I knew a lot of the actors who played the Muppet characters, and Miss Piggy and Kermit and I sang "Send in the Clowns" while a bunch of clown-clad Muppets danced behind us and the old men in the balcony chuffed and guffawed. The next song was "I Know an Old Lady Who Swallowed a Fly," and it went well, with Muppets again dancing all around me. Then there was a scene in a dressing room where a bomb goes off and smoke comes out of my costume. My fright at the sudden sound was very real, though I knew it was coming, and no one but me knew how close I had come to being annihilated by that little scene. I had no more songs in the show, and it was a good thing because, once again, the voice was gone. We all celebrated that it had "gone down a treat," as the English say. Only I knew how close I had come to losing it, and only I know, every time I see that show on YouTube, how close it came to being my last performance as a singer.

As soon as I got off the plane in New York I checked into Doctors Hospital under an assumed name and had the surgery to remove the hemangioma from my left vocal cord. The surgery was to be hush-hush, though Phil Donahue, during an interview a couple of years later, asked me on camera about the surgery on my vocal cords. I was more than surprised that he knew about the operation, but now I see it as a service. People should know that sometimes miracles happen. Dr. Weismann had taken a chance with a new procedure that had not yet been proven. He was able to give me my career back, and for that I will be eternally grateful.

When the dust settled I was still drinking and still

throwing up and still not knowing what I would do if I could not sing anymore. The thought would send bolts of terror through my body.

But I did recover, slowly. It would take nearly a year before I was totally healed and up to singing professionally again. I went to Weismann's office every week or so to see how the scar was coming along and tried some notes every few days to see if the voice was there at all. Before the end of 1977, I felt optimistic that in time I would be singing again. I prayed for the dream to come true, and it shimmered on the horizon.

I had a little money to see me through. I saw friends, went to therapy sessions, and tried to hold on to the relationship I had with Jerry. I would sometimes stay at his apartment downtown and finish off his vodka and then refill the bottle with water. I must have been totally out of it, since he liked a drink himself and would certainly know if he were not drinking the real thing. The relationship was shaky, and I think we were both deluded.

The winter dragged on into January of 1978, with no work and very little inspiration. I seldom had an uplifting thought or wrote a song or did much of anything but eat and sleep, drink and purge, and feel sorry for myself. This was not the Judy I knew. I was not a whiner, but I was in misery. During the big blizzard in January that year, I found myself one night on the subway going in the wrong direction. What a symbol of my life! I wound up in Harlem at midnight, lost and frightened, walking south toward my apartment on the Upper West Side, getting colder at every step, deeper in the falling snow. Things were getting worse by the day.

On March 2, 1978, without a fare-thee-well or a "Dear Judy" note, Jerry left, bicycle, typewriter, and all. I was totally devastated. And, of course, drunk. The bulimia was getting worse as well. God only knew when, or if, I would be able to stop doing either one. I certainly didn't, even when this career-threatening surgery overtook me. I knew I was going to have to deal with the alcoholism and the eating disorder. I wept and begged and humiliated myself on the phone. I told Jerry that I could not bear to lose him.

He stayed gone anyway.

There was more eating, more drinking, more bulimia, more sobbing, more long and ragged conversations with my sister, my friends, and my mother, who was as mad at Jerry as I was, I think. I felt I was being swept down the drain, lost in the river. I wanted to jump out of my high windows—no work, too fragile to sing yet, really, no voice to speak of, no joy, all loss, all misery all the time. I thought my life was over, finished. I kept trying to get myself back into shape, moderate my drinking, not eat too much, but it was not working.

It actually makes me weep to think I had no idea that I would be able to do what I do today, sing through sun and clouds, through thick and thin, stronger, more vibrant, clearer and better than ever.

Janet Matorin had been working for five years as my assistant and had gone through enormous ups and downs as my career soared into prominence, right down to having to cancel many shows during the previous year. I was not ready to sing and she knew I was in trouble and suggested we go to a fasting farm together. We packed up my blue Volvo station wagon and drove to Neversink, a weight-loss spa in the Catskills.

Neversink was a bare-bones place, but I had a sauna every day for ten days and sweated out the booze. I had sleeping pills, downers, and other mood-altering drugs. I had pockets, purses, drawers full of every kind of medication on offer from my fancy Upper East Side doctors, who all thought I was so successful that I could not possibly be an alcoholic and I certainly did not have an eating disorder because I was so normal-looking. They would give me prescriptions for anything I asked for. So even though I was not eating or drinking, I was getting high! I lost ten pounds at Neversink, and when I got back home I tore into the food that was in my kitchen and put back half of the weight in two days. That is compulsive eating, a machine that never stops, even if you have just come back from a fasting farm and lost those ten ugly pounds.

And the desperation in my drinking and bulimia simply increased. The dark was hunkering closer to my windows, which looked out over the Hudson River. I wanted to drown, I wanted to die. I knew I had to do something about my life. I was going down fast.

The only person I really knew who was an alcoholic who no longer drank was my friend the composer Ned Rorem. Brilliant and famous, a writer of scintillating memoirs and exquisite songs and symphonies, he had gone to AA and stopped drinking years earlier in Paris. I would visit him in his apartment on the Upper West Side and go to his parties attended by other composers and musicians such as Leonard Bernstein and David Diamond. I would drink Ned's French liqueurs (kept for parties and those who drank, like me), and he would tell me all about how he got sober in an Anonymous program. One night in January I asked him to take me to an AA meeting in a church on Lexington and Eightieth street. Stumbling and incoherent, but dazzled by the meeting and the stories, I was in tears and flooded with agony because I thought it was wonderful and knew it was beyond my reach, an impossible dream.

I once heard a story about one of our friends who was an untreated alcoholic and who was taken to an AA meeting by a longtime member. After the meeting the longtimer asked the visitor what he thought of the meeting.

"I thought it was one of the most amazing things I have ever witnessed—thrilling, really. Everyone who spoke was eloquent and moving, and I was in tears half the time. I was lifted right out of my chair. I couldn't believe how honest everyone who spoke was, how touching."

The longtimer then asked the newcomer if he would go to another meeting.

"Never!"

Like the newcomer, I went home thinking, "It's very good for them, they really needed it." I was not so sure about myself. Honestly, I was so sick I didn't hear the message that was meant for me.

I had been participating in the National Dance Institute's annual performance at Lincoln Center for a few years by then. Jacques d'Amboise, a principal dancer with George Balanchine's City Ballet, had founded the institute, whose purpose was to train boys for ballet. NDI brought in students from area schools and taught them (eventually girls as well as boys) in classes at Lincoln Center on Saturday mornings. Many of these kids were from underprivileged backgrounds and were saved from the streets and the beckoning of crime and drugs by the classes that Jacques and his teachers gave for the dancers. Many took to the dance floor with a spirit and a will that was inspiring. Every year I would write songs for and sing in the show and at the end of each year's performance the kids—up to a thousand of them—would dance the finale. I told Jacques I wanted to dance with them as well (I no longer smoked and was running every day), saying that all the guests on the show should be dancing with the kids. By then Jacques even had a dozen New York City policemen dancing in the finale, and he told me if I was serious I had to start coming to his wife's dance class.

I was going to learn to dance at last! Even in my

disjointed and depressed state, I looked forward to the classes. Moving my body in a different way than my usual workouts—and I never stopped working out—might make a difference in the way I was feeling.

I joined Carolyn d'Amboise's classes, and sweated and worked out through as many hangovers as I could. At my first class, I met a woman who was one of the strongest supporters of the NDI. I knew she was married to a famous actor, whose career was thriving. He was also a well-known and photogenic drinker who appeared from time to time on the cover of the *Daily News* in the process of being thrown out of some bar, blood-spattered, angry, and lunging across a room full of overturned tables and chairs, or chasing after his quarry, some poor soul who was afraid of the movie star stumbling through the White Horse Tavern or the Lion's Head. I had been proudly aware of this actor saying to the world, "I will do this the way I planned and no one can stop me." And so I was vaguely puzzled when I stopped seeing his handsome, grimacing, bloody face looking out at me from the pages of the New York dailies.

I called my new friend to ask her what had happened to her husband. "He stopped drinking," she said. I must have registered shock. "Would you like to talk to him? I am sure he would want to speak to you." She gave me her husband's phone number. He was on a movie set in Arizona, she said.

So that night I called him and we talked for about

forty minutes. He was so loving and kind, and listened with attention as I told my story—one of drinking myself into oblivion day after day, year after year. I made no mention of my eating disorder. Even my therapist did not know of this horror. It would be my secret till the grave, I was sure. He told me I had to see Dr. Stanley Gitlow, one of the few doctors anywhere in the country who understood and was able to help the alcoholic. He had found Gitlow, and his life was totally changed.

If this doctor was good enough for this famous actor, he was good enough for me. Though I did not really believe it at the time, I was actually ready to be helped.

The next day I called Gitlow's office and made an appointment. And so it was, on Fifth Avenue, in the middle of April, that I got confirmation that I was going to die if I didn't get help. He understood. It helped that he was wearing a white coat. He said I had a disease that would kill me if it were not treated and put me on the phone with Chit Chat Farms, a rehab center in the beautiful hills of Pennsylvania. I made arrangements to attend their twenty-eight-day program. I would arrive on April 19—four days away.

Gitlow wanted me to go from his office to Pennsylvania, but I told him I had promised that I would attend a fund-raiser for the Equal Rights Amendment that very night and I was not going to let them down.

I would be joining Stephen Sondheim, Bella Abzug, Gloria Steinem, and a number of other stars at the party.

I invited my old friend Jeanne Livingston, who had decorated my Upper West Side apartment and held my hand during my descent into alcoholic and bulimic hell, listened to my drunken monologues, taken me to lunches and dinners, and come to get me after my surgery for the hemangioma. She had just started dating Bob Gerson, a well-known industrial designer, and wanted me to meet his partner, Louis Nelson. Jeanne is also an astrologer and had done our charts. She told me Louis was a Libra and would go well with me, a Taurus. I told her to, in a word, forget it. I was too broken up over Jerry and could not think straight and certainly did not want to go on a date.

"So," she said, "I will bring him to the party. Louis can be your blind date." She told me he was handsome, kind, brilliant, and a gentleman. I came to my senses and gave in.

I put on a silk dress that still fit, applied makeup, and combed my hair, and felt lifted by a breeze as I stepped out onto West End Avenue and got into a cab that took me downtown to the fund-raiser. Inside, I was taken around the room to meet the other guests and pose for pictures, all the while keeping my eye out for Jeanne and my blind date. Louis always says it was blind for me but not for him, since he knew exactly who I was. When Jeanne showed up with Louis, she introduced us and we sat together. Louis was handsome, she was right. And he had bright blue eyes. I liked him immediately, and we talked easily. I introduced him to everyone at the party.

We got on well and he saw me home in a cab. He walked me to my door, shook my hand, and said he would like to see me again. I was indeed smitten.

During the next two days I called Louis a couple of times and we talked as though we had always known each other. But I did not tell him I was going away to get sober. I was not sure about that, anyway.

Aside from the evening at the fund-raiser, my illness had made it nearly impossible for me to work or even to show up for anything much of the time. Janet and my accountant, two people who were still answering my phone calls, and who were willing to see that I got some help, flew with me to Reading, Pennsylvania, on April 19, 1978. They watched me deplane before they flew back to New York. I was met at baggage claim by a tall young man in jeans who carried my luggage—two huge bags of clothes, a typewriter, and a heavy suitcase of books—to a low-slung station wagon. I was in a daze as he drove me in silence to the farm in Wernersville, where the flowers were blooming. I arrived at Chit Chat, a beautiful little white-columned Revolutionary-style house surrounded by trees and rolling hills, very drunk, having started my morning at home with a few shots of vodka and had my last drink out of a jelly jar in the bath-room of the Reading airport. I checked in, was given a room with a roommate who got down on her knees before bed at night and early in the morning. I found the sight revolting. Within a few days of arriving at Chit

Chat, I, too, was on my knees, a woman detoxing from booze and trying to get sober.

I was given a job working on the garbage truck with Ralph—I drove, and Ralph slung the garbage cans onto the pickup. We told each other our stories and laughed at our bungled alcoholic lives. In the meetings at night, I laughed more. I was shocked to be laughing at my own and others' terrible stories, some of them tragic, but there, with Ralph and sixty other recovering drunks, I began to get better, to get sober. Mealtimes were shared experiences, where the food was abundant and delicious. And after each meal, I went to a bathroom and threw up.

I got lucky, the demons were lifted—at least the booze demon. I was there for four weeks. I came home to New York a new woman, with clear eyes and a sober heart and a body that did not crave alcohol. My life was totally changed. It was a miracle.

But I was still fighting the food. I lost some weight but was still bulimic. I was thin, and healthy in many ways, but I was still purging as I had been for eight years. My sobriety was rooted in an Anonymous program, and after getting sober I devoted myself to the (seemingly!) simple plan of not drinking and going to meetings of like-minded people who were recovering. I stuck with the winners. I started to sing, to work, to focus, to thrive. The blackness that had been my drinking history resolved itself in a kind of bright and fantastic light, another dimension of living.

But my eating disorder had to be dealt with. I soon

found that for anything that might ail you, there is an Anonymous program. And food and eating disorders were addictions that could be and were being addressed by one Anonymous program or another.

Father Joseph C. Martin, the great doctor who helped so many alcoholics to sobriety through his personal recovery and the work of his rehabilitation center, and whose movie *Chalk Talk on Alcohol* I saw in the first week of treatment at Chit Chat, says alcoholism is a treatable illness. He also says alcoholism is an illness driven by an allergy. The allergy, he says, comes when alcohol (which usually is made of fermented grain, rice, potatoes, barley, or corn) enters the body of an alcoholic and sets up a compulsion to have more of the same substance. My body, which is at 98.6 degrees Fahrenheit most of the time, makes me a walking brewery when I eat the foods that make up alcohol—grains, sugar, potatoes, corn, flour, barley—and since I am allergic to these foods, the allergy sets up the obsession.

When I start, I cannot stop. I never mentioned my bulimia and food addiction during the time I was at Chit Chat. I got sober and stayed sober, but I would be throwing up for another three years.

One nightmare was over, and the other was just warming up.

CHAPTER 19

LIVES OF THE DIET GURUS

The Scarsdale Diet and Dr. Herman Tarnower

The fruits eaten temperately need not make us ashamed
of our appetites, nor interrupt the worthiest pursuits.
But put an extra condiment into your dish, and it will
poison you.

—DAVID HENRY THOREAU, *WALDEN*

In the 1970s, we meet Dr. Herman Tarnower, another
cardiologist. He was a champion of ideas popularized
by Banting, Donaldson, Pennington, Atkins, Taller, and
others who recommended a diet low in carbohydrates,
salt, and sugar, and encouraged lean meat, oily fish, fruit,
and vegetables.

Tarnower was the son of a prosperous milliner in New
York. His well-off family provided him with the sheen of
civility and culture. Tarnower went to Syracuse University for his undergraduate degree as well as his medical

training, and at the start of World War II, he joined the U.S. Army Medical Corps, where he was promoted to the rank of major. He was stationed in Japan and developed a love of Japanese art. After the war he settled in Scarsdale, New York, where he founded the Scarsdale Medical Group in the 1950s.

In the living room of his upscale home, the heads of many wild animals, trophies of hunting expeditions in Africa and the Far East, were displayed along with his collection of guns and statues of Buddha he had gathered on his many trips. In the garden that surrounded his home, a life-size Buddha, covered in a carapace of crackled gold, greeted visitors with stoic serenity.

Tarnower's dietary fame and renown evolved from a one-page typed list of food choices that he mimeographed and handed out regularly to his cardiac patients. These were not suggestions. When *The Complete Scarsdale Medical Diet* was published in 1978, it became an instant bestseller, was featured on radio and television, and made Tarnower not only rich but famous. Jean Harris, the headmistress of an exclusive boarding school for girls, and with whom Tarnower was having an affair, is thanked in the preface of his first book, indicating that she had some input in its writing. There were many high-profile personalities who emerged to praise both the diet and Tarnower; even the president of Bloomingdale's gave the diet an enthusiastic endorsement, saying he had lost weight and found it totally effective.

Behind the slick, well-designed cover, Tarnower presented a rigid two-week approach to dieting. It is a simple plan:

BREAKFAST

· Half of a grapefruit, or if they're unavailable,
  ½ cup diced fresh pineapple or ½ mango or
  ½ papaya or ½ cantaloupe or a generous slice of
  honeydew, casaba or other available melon
· Slice of whole meal or protein toast (no spreads
  or butter)
· Coffee (no sugar or milk)

LUNCH

· Canned tuna
· Salad (lettuce, tomato, cucumbers, and celery)
  with oil-free dressing
· Coffee, tea, diet soda, or water

DINNER

· Roast lamb (with all visible fat removed) or fish,
  seafood, chicken, turkey, or vegetable protein

- Salad with lemon and vinegar dressing
- Coffee

In the daily regimen the dieter is encouraged not to make substitutions. Tarnower also urged his patients to walk three miles a day—whether they needed to or not. The diet was a great success and Tarnower's life seemed blessed—that is, until he was murdered by the woman he was jilting for another lover. His death would become far more prominent than his diet, at least for a while.

Along with his expertise in medicine and big-game hunting, Tarnower was said to have another hobby: collecting beautiful women. In 1966, thirteen years before he published his famous diet, Tarnower met Jean Struver Harris, the headmistress at that time of the Thomas School for Boys. Harris was born in Cleveland, had graduated magna cum laude from Smith College, and was well known in Tarnower's circle of friends. When they met, she was divorced from her first husband, with whom she had two sons, David and James. Tarnower had never married, and when he fell in love with Harris it looked like the real thing. For a few years, they seemed to have a good relationship, traveling abroad together, socializing, both working hard and enjoying their careers. At the time that Tarnower began to consider publishing a book about his diet, Harris left the Thomas School and was hired by the Madeira School for Girls in McLean, Virginia. With its 100 percent college admission record,

Madeira was considered one of the best private boarding schools for girls in the country. Founded in 1906 by Miss Lucy Madeira, the motto of the school was "Function in disaster, finish in style." Harris was chosen from a hundred candidates and the fit between her and the school could not have seemed more perfect.

She was devoted to her job and would often teach what she called her "integrity" speech, focusing on the values for which young women should strive. The school seemed to enhance the talents of those who passed through its doors and many of Madeira's students went on to great success; Katharine Graham, who would take over as publisher of *The Washington Post* after her husband's death, was a student, as were, in later years, the daughters of both Sam Donaldson and Eric Sevareid, as well as a Rockefeller granddaughter.

In 1977, Tarnower started an affair with Lynne Tryforos, an assistant at the Scarsdale Medical Group; she was helping with the publication of *The Complete Scarsdale Medical Diet*. She was twenty years younger than Harris. By now, Harris and Tarnower had been together a dozen years. He had always refused to marry Jean, and the affair with Tryforos left Harris stranded in the upper reaches of her own destiny—jilted by the diet doctor.

At first Harris seemed able to take Tarnower's betrayal in stride. She proceeded in her usual calm and professional manner. Tarnower continued to see both women, as though variety were the spice of his life, taking Tryforos on overseas trips, having her to dinner at his home with other friends (who had previously also been friends of Harris and Tarnower), but going on vacations with Harris as well. He even took out a birthday greeting ad to Tryforos in *The New York Times*. A friend told Harris about it. "Why don't you just rent the Goodyear blimp? I think it's available," Harris was reported to have told the doctor.

But eventually, the calm, intelligent headmistress seemed to be turning into a nervous wreck, scratching her head, biting her nails, and losing her temper with staff and students alike. She began to stress her "integrity" speech even more vehemently, and to take severe actions for incursions of misbehavior. Young women previously in awe of her began to accuse her of being short, curt, "a cold fish," inflexible. Her dismissal of four students for having marijuana seeds and stems in their room fanned a virtual fire of protest, and by 1980 a real scandal had erupted, as most students and parents sided against Harris. A movement began to have her fired. There were protesters in front of the Madeira School carrying signs demanding Harris's resignation and shouting for her to come out and face the music. At first she hid in her office, and then, a scarf over her hair and her car keys in her hand, she sneaked out a back door and into her car.

Tarnower was planning to celebrate his birthday that very night with Tryforos and other friends at his home. Harris was not invited and certainly not expected. As she drove in a raging rainstorm to Tarnower's house, she described herself as feeling hysterical, knowing she was probably going to lose her job. She would later tell doctors and lawyers alike that she was in despair, totally unhinged.

The descriptions Harris gave later of her mood were of a woman clearly out of her mind. She was armed with a gun when she burst through the front door of Tarnower's home. She and the doctor fell to arguing at once about his affair as she swore she was going to kill herself. Harris fled at one point to the bathroom and found there what she knew to be Tryforos's lingerie, jewelry, and purse. Racing back into the living room, she screamed again that she was going to use the gun on herself.

Tarnower shouted at her as she railed at him, waving a gun in his face while he tried to calm her down. She shot him four times at close range and he fell dead at her feet. Statues of the Buddha and heads of wild animals were the only other witnesses to Tarnower's death.

When the police came (Harris had called 911), she kept saying, "I did it, I killed him." She was taken into custody, then released on $40,000 bail and sent for a psychiatric evaluation. The trial in White Plains lasted fourteen weeks and was said to be one of the longest in New York history. In the end Harris was convicted of second-degree murder and sentenced to fifteen years in prison.

For many years it was unclear exactly how much Harris had to do with the structure of the Scarsdale diet, or if Tryforos had made a contribution to either the diet or the book. But in the ninth edition, the publisher put questions to rest on both issues; the acknowledgments page declares: "We are grateful to Jean Harris for her splendid assistance in the research and writing of this book." And two paragraphs later, "We wish, especially, to thank Lynne Tryforos."

Governor Mario Cuomo pardoned Harris in 1993. In the fourteen years she was incarcerated in the women's prison in Westchester, there were endless pleas for her release, while sales of *The Complete Scarsdale Medical Diet* soared. During her prison term Harris made great efforts on behalf of women who were prisoners, resulting in much better treatment for them, especially by helping mothers get better visiting rights with their children.

It always makes me think that when the heart and rage and a firearm do the dance of death that this could have been me, there in that house on that rainy night among the Buddhas and the stuffed heads of wild animals, full of grief and the poison of envy and jealousy. Many times there were hot flashes of hurt and possible blood and death around me. I thank God I never owned a gun, because I most certainly would have used it.

Jean Harris died at eighty-nine on December 23, 2012.

CHAPTER 20

MY JOURNEY

Life on Life's Terms

Follow your Bliss. I say, follow your bliss and don't be afraid.

—JOSEPH CAMPBELL

I got home from Chit Chat at the beginning of May 1978, after detox and four weeks of treatment. I had just turned thirty-nine. I understood that I had a disease that is cunning, baffling, powerful, and seductive. It is an illness that is spiritual, physical, emotional, and mental, and is driven by an addiction in the body to the substance of alcohol and the ingredients of which it is made. I was sober, shaky, fragile, and terrified that I would drink again. But I also knew that the game was over and the prize was in hand. I might have to fight for it for all I was worth, but I was not going back to the nightmare that I had been living before Chit Chat, before the program, before the light dawned on this fried brain of mine.

32

But I was still purging and had not yet fallen to the bottom of the well with my eating disorder.

When I had about two months of sobriety, I got a call from Jeanne Livingston, who asked me what was going on with Louis Nelson. He was interested in me, she said, and I should call him. So I did, and on July 10, a beautiful summer evening, Louis and I met at Orsini's, an Italian restaurant on Fifty-sixth Street. He was waiting at a table by the window overlooking the street. White lace curtains blew softly around the windows, and as I walked across the red tile floor toward his table I saw those bright blue eyes and that wide-open smile greeting me. I cocked my head and he smiled back, and as I sat down, I thought, Oh, this man is very handsome and very charming. And we were off to the rest of the evening talking about everything.

I had already told him when I had called him what I had done, where I had been.

"Don't you know your entire life will change now?" he said. And change it did.

Louis is an industrial designer who grew up in New York, went to Brooklyn Tech and the Pratt Institute, and spent a few years in the army flying helicopters in Germany and training helicopter pilots. He returned for his master's to Pratt, where he was an assistant to Rowena Reed Kostellow, a cofounder of the industrial design department. He started his career as a designer for Corning Glass and later formed a partnership with Bob Gerson in New York in the 1970s. Louis has designed everything from World Expos in many countries; to the brightly colored skis that took the Head Ski company, famous for its black, sleek ski, into rainbow colors; to the Nutritional Facts panels that appear on all packaged foods. In the early 1990s he would also design the mural of portraits at the Korean War Memorial on the Mall in Washington, D.C.

We started dating, and soon were living together. We had a wonderful life from the first. There were problems but we got through them. We were both in therapy, which helped. I was so happy and, of course, sober, and life was so different. The drama was at a low ebb; I would say it was nearly gone. And the adventures we had were great—trips to Colorado, where Clark and my family and Louis's joined us. I had started working again a few months after we met, making new albums and playing concerts all over the world.

I was truly sober but I was still drunk with the food.

In August 1978 when I was four months sober, Antonia Brico came through New York on her way to the music festivals in Europe. For many years, she and I would have lunch at the Russian Tea Room on her visits, but now, shiny and new like a freshly polished Daimler Princess, I was sober. We sat down for lunch and she said, "I love your hair back like that" (instead of down around my face, scraggly and drooping). I thanked her.

Over borscht and Russian cream, I got up the courage

to ask Brico a question I had always been too shy to ask, about the portrait on the table by her piano so many years before of a bearded guru, which I had seen when my team and I were shooting *Antonia: A Portrait of the Woman*. In a room that was filled with statues of Beethoven, Bach, Casals, and other musicians, I had wondered who in the world was in this little picture in an oval frame, this bearded and wise-looking man on her table.

She was quiet for a while and then she asked me if I knew what Kriya Yoga was. I said I didn't. She told me to get a book called *Autobiography of a Yogi* and read it. It was the story of her guru, the man in the picture.

I had always been looking for the right meditation during all those years I was drinking and eating my way to oblivion. I had met the Maharishi once and felt his powerful faith and that even the flowers around him were filled with peace. In the sixties I went to hear Krish-namurti speak at the New School and had an out-of-body experience in which I floated through the next few days, unable to pull myself back to earth, flying like the people who inexplicably levitate while meditating. I read much of Thomas Merton and prayed in church, built myself little pedestals on which I put flowers and candles.

Now Brico had given me directions. I went to a bookstore and bought *Autobiography of a Yogi* and began reading. I was instantly enthralled. In its pages I learned about Kriya Yoga and about Paramahansa Yogananda, and found my path to meditation. I went to the Self-

Realization Fellowship Center in Los Angeles, which teaches Yogananda's yoga and meditation, and met the woman who had taken over his foundation when he died in 1952. It was Daya Mata who told me the story of how Yogananda had come into her life through Brico, who had become a devotee of the guru in New York in 1921. The guru had helped Brico go to Germany to study conducting. He told her not to listen to those who said she could not be a conductor. He helped her find her dream and make it come true.

Brico had never, in all the years I had known her, mentioned her spiritual life or Yogananda and the amazing story of how she found him.

"Who knows does not tell," she would say later. "And who tells does not know."

Still, I tell, since I want you to know. Ever since I went to California in the early 1980s and took my instruction with the nuns and with Daya Mata at the Self-Realization Center in Los Angeles, I have done this form of meditation, sometimes perfectly, sometimes imperfectly. Kriya Yoga has answered my every question about how to meditate and it keeps me on the path of light and joy, healing and happiness.

Perhaps this newfound meditation helped me do something about my bulimia, for, in early 1979, sober for about a year, I started going to Anonymous food programs to find a solution. I had been bulimic for eight years by that time. I went to meetings, wrote down and called in my food consumption to my sponsor, did the suggested steps—a lot of writing, reading, meditating— and still could not stop bingeing and purging.

I learned some better habits, yes. I knew what to eat and what not to eat; these first years in the Anonymous programs taught me that. But I was in psychic pain, and desperate for this to work. If I could get sober, why couldn't I get abstinent from bulimia?

One day, after nearly four years of struggle, on December 4, 1982, I was again desperate. Louis was away working. I was bingeing like a maniac on my favorites—always carbs, sugar, flour—the usual suspects, the things we have trouble putting down, having only one of. I had been to the bakery and the market. I came home with Almond Joys, Mars bars, Rice Krispies cookies, glazed doughnuts, fruit bread, sugared walnuts. I could binge on Japanese food, on rice. I ate everything in sight. I must have had five purges that day, and I was bleary-eyed and sick to my soul. I wanted to walk in front of a bus.

It was a Saturday. I had no concert. I was home alone. I headed out the door to find a meeting I thought was in a church on Ninety-sixth between Broadway and Amsterdam. When I got there I wandered from door to door and found all were locked. I got a taxi and headed south, to another meeting for alcoholics on East Eighty-fourth Street. There, in the dark and soothing space inside the church, where the alcove was filled with both friends and strangers who had one of the problems I had but not the one I was so desperate about, I found the solution. In among the shadows and light of the undercroft I spotted the bright, shining face of a woman I knew. I had been told she had a food problem and I had been avoiding calling her for months. Now, desperate, I approached her after the meeting and spilled out my story of despair and frustration. I told her that I simply could not get abstinent from bulimia.

Ann smiled her beautiful smile and said, "Are you ready to do anything?" I said I was. Not believing it but saying it. "Put on your coat, we are going to York and Seventy-fourth."

To another church we went, to another meeting. This one was the same type of Anonymous food program I had been going to, just a new location for me. We sat, listening to inspiring speakers, and after the meeting Ann picked out a pamphlet from the literature table that was called "Dignity of Choice." It was a list of seven food plans.

"You are on number one, what's called the GreySheet, and you are going to stay on it. No end in sight." She wrote out what I could have for breakfast, lunch, and dinner the next day. I had been keeping my weight down with the bulimia so I weighed only 125, but to me I seemed huge, a hulking, walking eating machine. The only thing that stood between me and the huge-size clothes I might have had to wear was a ferocious, constant, agonizing, and total control, and an overriding fear of gaining weight. It was destroying me.

I went home, stopping to buy the things I would need for my meals the next day. In a phone call I told Louis what my plan was. (I had not yet admitted to him that I was bulimic. It was my dirty little secret even from him.)

The next day, December 5, 1982, after eleven straight years of active bulimia, I got up, had my coffee (bless my coffee), and ate my breakfast of tofu, fruit, and soy milk. I knew after I'd had my breakfast (and I had not eaten a proper breakfast for years) that the game—and the bulimia—was over, never to return.

How did I know that? How did that happen? I had eaten a great breakfast, and I knew I had two more wonderful meals coming that day. I had a big salad with dressing and four ounces of protein for lunch; I had a great dinner of grilled chicken, my favorite to this day, a salad with dressing, and vegetables. It was more than enough, and delicious and abundant.

But I was still a little crazy in the head. A year and a half into the Anonymous food program I remained on the Anonymous plan number one, but I was also playing with food and decided I should eat no salt at all. I knew that would get me down to the 110 weight I longed for. One night I passed out at home and couldn't get off the floor. Louis was in California on business again. I reached the phone and called my assistant, who called 911. The

EMTs came and could not bring my blood pressure up (think Karen Carpenter). They took me to the hospital and I was given an IV of salt water. My personal physician said, "Eat a little salt with your meals."

But my sponsor Ann had other ideas. There were seven food plans in the program, and after the first (the Grey-Sheet), there were plans that included carbs and other foods.

I knew that the GreySheet had stopped my bulimia cold. When it was suggested I add other foods I felt as though a knife had cut me to the core. But I complied. I went on to the other diets where eventually I could have a little of this, a little of that. I was becoming a "normal" eater.

But I did not know what a "normal meal" was. I did the best I could. I no longer binged, no longer purged. I went to meetings and kept my food journals. I was happy and in remission.

Thank God Louis and my son were getting along beautifully. Clark had been in trouble with drugs for a long time, but when he finally came home to New York from private schools and was living with me in 1977, his life turned around. He graduated from Saint Ann's in Brooklyn and by the time I was a couple of years sober and living with Louis, Clark had started college and was in his own apartment and having his own life. He moved to Providence shortly after I met Louis and had moved in with the wonderful Amy Wagner, whom he said was the love of his life. She said the same of him. But his heroin addiction grabbed him again and was taking him through hell, and me and Louis and the rest of our family along with him.

Louis, who adored Clark, was a witness to all of the drama and anxiety. Clark was living a dangerous, drug-filled, drug-dealing existence, and now Amy fled the scene. The calls I got and the times we spent worrying about Clark—was he going to live or die—were terrifying.

One foggy February morning in 1984, I got the call I was waiting for. It was Clark, saying he was ready to go into treatment. I arranged for him to go to Hazelden, the granddaddy of all rehabs, and he went. Finally the fog and the pain and the horror lifted; he was sober and making a good life in St. Paul, with a splendid support system, good friends, and a great sponsor. My old friend from Colorado, Terry Williams, helped Clark so much in those years. Louis and I went out to visit and Clark came to New York to see us. In 1987 he brought his new love to meet us. Alyson and Clark married and had a beautiful little girl, Hollis, in October 1987. We were beside ourselves with joy for my son and his wife and baby.

The years went by with visits and celebrations, vacations together in Minnesota and Colorado and New York. I thought every problem was solved. My concerts and recordings were going well. It seemed I was living in a dream come true.

We know that drug addiction and alcoholism are diseases, and people with diseases sometimes relapse. It happened to my son in November 1991, when he had nearly seven years of sobriety. Everyone has problems, and some of them are intolerable, and some make people drink, however long they are sober, however much they long to stay sober. Relapse is one of the baffling things about the illness, and I never thought it could happen to my son or me. I was so wrong, terribly, heartbreakingly wrong.

I had been out to visit Clark and his family a week before his relapse, and though I knew he was struggling with personal issues having to do with his marriage, I was sure he was going to get back into recovery. He lived in the renowned home of recovery, after all: St. Paul, Minnesota, where every other person is either a recovering addict or bound for Center City to go into treatment. There are meetings galore in St. Paul. I had been to many of them with Clark, and knew that he was surrounded with loving, caring, sober people, some of whom were his close friends, most of whom he could confide in. I just did not think the many-eyed monster of alcoholism had the power to invade our private dream, our happy time, and our joyful story.

You can look back, but you can't stare. We all were doing our best, trying to help. It was not to be on my terms.

We talked a few times when Clark was in the Renewal Center, where he had gone for a week of contemplation, writing, and discussing his progress with people who knew the illness, and again on January 10, a couple of days after his birthday, to discuss my upcoming visit: I would be flying out to see him the next weekend.

I had a few days off and was looking forward to seeing him. He sounded good, very up and hopeful. He said he was sober and things were going to be fine. I knew he and Alyson had had some problems, but hoped that everything was going to be resolved.

"I love you, Mom" were his last words to me. I tried to reach him on January 13 and 14 to confirm my arrival time. I could not find him. I kept trying the morning of January 15, to no avail. I just expected he would meet me at the airport in three days as planned.

Late that afternoon, my doorbell rang. I opened the door to my brother Denver John, who was ashen-faced. I was screaming because I already knew why he was at my door that late in the day. He took me in his arms and told me my son was dead.

Louis was in Washington, D.C., for a big meeting with the architects for the Korean War Veterans Memorial. Louis had been awarded the commission to design the memorial along with the sculptor Frank Gaylord, and work had already begun on plans for its construction. He caught a plane from D.C. and flew to St. Paul, where we met.

Clark's death was the saddest moment of my life. I kissed his beautiful face for the last time at the mortuary before they dispatched his body to the flames, ashes to ashes. At the funeral were Terry and Trish, Clark's close friends and confidants; my mother and siblings, Holly, David, Denver John, and Michael; Clark's father, Peter, Aunt Hadley, and Uncle Gary; and dozens of Clark's friends from St. Paul. His beautiful little four-year-old daughter, Hollis, carried the roses and threw them onto the casket, and her mother, Alyson, and all of our friends wept and sang songs and shared stories about this funny, sweet, unforgettable redhead, son and friend, father and grandson. Many in the family spoke of the suicide of Clark's grandfather on his father's side, Gary Alan Taylor, who had committed suicide in the same way, with carbon monoxide poisoning, in his car in the garage.

I sang "Amazing Grace" and prayed and wept. My granddaughter did not understand why her father was gone. I was sure I would die from this wild grief.

But I did not die, though every day I thought I might. I knew that I could not drink, that if I did I would certainly be lost, like my son. I also could not eat, not for weeks.

My weight plummeted. It was friends, and prayer, and suicide recovery groups, and my beloved husband Louis who went through every moment with me, who helped me get through those terrible days. Joan Rivers called me the day I got back from the funeral and said, "I know you want to stop everything, cancel all your shows." I said I already had. "You can't do that, I know because I have been there. You have to work, you will not heal if you

don't. You will never get over this if you stop working."
She knew what she was talking about. Her husband and
the father of her daughter, Melissa, had killed himself
five years earlier, and she had worked her way out of her
rage and heartache. Joan was right, of course, and I took
her advice.

I rescheduled all the shows I had canceled, and I went
out on the road. Louis came to California with me. My
mother traveled with me to Minnesota, a sad trip for
her, distraught and broken with her own grief; my sister, Holly, brought her one-year-old, Aidan, to Arizona
from California, and we wept together in the desert and
laughed together over my nephew's antics, a healing
grace I needed desperately. I felt some angel's wings pass
over us. This has happened to other people, not just me.
Not just my sister, my family, my brothers, my son and
his friends. My granddaughter. The healing would come
and go, lifting me up for an hour or so before the dark
came back again. It was like that for a long, long time.

Many spouses cannot stay the course after such an
assault to the sanity and serenity of a family that a suicide or other traumatic death may bring. Louis stayed the
course, wept with me, held me, prayed with me, and supported me. Slowly I started to be able to breathe, to eat.
Louis helped me live through Clark's death. We went to
survival groups, talked about life and death with friends,
made our way through the first days, the first weeks, the

first year of this terrible loss. He mourned with me and stayed through the bad as he has through the good.

There has not been a day since that I have not mourned Clark or wished he were here with me. Hollis is here, strong and wise and solid, a mother herself. She is a wonderful mother to her baby, who smiles most of the time, like his mother does. Like his grandfather did.

But miracles keep happening all around us along with tragedy, no matter what. I did not drink, and four years after Clark's death, and after eighteen years of a committed partnership, Louis and I were married in a beautiful service at the Cathedral of Saint John the Divine in 1996.

I was very thin, and I was happy.

CHAPTER 21

Bill Wilson and Dr. Bob Smith—Alcoholism and Food Addiction

The odds of going to the store for a loaf of bread and coming out with only a loaf of bread are three billion to one.

—ERMA BOMBECK

The Anonymous programs I speak about in these pages have been used to help millions of alcoholics as well as overeaters, bulimics, anorexics, and the morbidly obese. Gambling addicts, narcotics addicts, sex addicts, and families and friends of addicts have received priceless help—free to all, supported by contributions only—from the original *Twelve Steps and Twelve Traditions* and *The Big Book of Alcoholics Anonymous*. According to research, today there are more than three hundred groups that use the Alcoholics Anonymous route to healthy living, including a group called Mistresses Anonymous.

In 1935, Bill Wilson and Dr. Bob Smith got together in Akron, Ohio, and started the program that would eventually save millions of lives and restore drunks (and all kinds of addicts) to sanity and society.

The man who would eventually become the co-founder of AA was Bill Wilson, a New York stockbroker who was down on his luck. A sick alcoholic, he knew his drinking was killing him. Wilson was afraid he might throw himself down the stairs in his home, or out a window, and had been trying to get sober for years, checking himself into Towns Hospital in Manhattan for a few days a couple of times a year and within weeks going back to his old ways. During Wilson's last stay at Towns in 1934, Dr. William Silkworth, the hospital's medical director, told him his case was hopeless.

"You people are heartbreaking," the doctor said. "I can't help you. Don't come back. "

A few days later, Wilson was again drinking around the clock when his old friend Ebby Thacher called to say he would like to stop by. Wilson had known Thacher as a hard drinker like himself, but his friend arrived at the Wilsons' home a changed man. He was sober. He told Wilson about the Oxford Group, which held meetings at Calvary Church in New York City, and said he had found an answer to his drinking.

Instead of the friendly drunk Wilson had known in the past, Thacher was now clear-eyed, filled with energy, and speaking of God. It disgusted Wilson, who had no use for such talk. But after Thacher left, Wilson found himself wondering about the things Thacher had told him, and what might have changed his friend's lifelong drinking habits. Thacher had shared the six steps that members in the Oxford Group practice:

1. Admitted we were hopeless
2. Got honest with ourselves
3. Got honest with another
4. Made amends
5. Helped others without demand
6. Prayed to God as we understood Him

Started by the missionary Frank Buchman in 1931, the Oxford Group had "no hierarchy, no temples, no endowments; its workers had no salaries, and no plans but God's plan." Still skeptical, Wilson nonetheless made a few visits to Calvary Church with Thacher and met some of the members of the Oxford Group. He called Dr. Silkworth and begged to be allowed to come back for another detox at Towns Hospital. Silkworth took him in again, doubtful but unable to turn his old patient away—maybe this man had found something—and Wilson detoxed for the last time.

During that stay at Towns, Wilson had a spiritual experience that would help him find his way into a life free of the demon alcohol and would inspire others to follow the same path to sobriety.

Wilson got active, going to Calvary Church, talking to other men about how he had been able to stay sober. He spoke of a sudden spiritual experience. He returned to his job as a stockbroker, reconnecting with clients in the business in which he'd had previous success. When he had been sober for six months, talking to other drunks, he became discouraged. He told his wife, Lois, that the men he had tried to help were not getting sober. Lois pulled him up short, saying that he had better keep on doing what he was doing, since he himself had actually been able to stay sober.

In June 1935, Wilson made a trip to Akron, Ohio, to close a stock margin deal. The deal went south, and he desperately wanted to drink. Instead, he picked up the telephone next to the bar in the basement of the May-flower Hotel where he was staying. He thought if he could reach out to a local church and ask if anyone knew someone he could help with his story, he might be able to stay sober.

All the first numbers were busy or did not answer. But the last name on the list was a Reverend Walter F. Tunks, whose friend Henrietta Seiberling answered the phone. When Wilson explained to her what he was seeking— another drunk to talk to—she told him she knew just such a person, Dr. Bob Smith, and arranged for them to meet.

The next afternoon, what was planned as a ten-minute conversation between the two men ended up lasting well into the middle of the night, becoming the bedrock of the Anonymous programs—people who had little in common other than their addictions talking to each other and sharing their stories. Instead of the preacher, the doctor, and the expert telling people they should stop doing what they were doing, condemning their lack of discipline and moral fiber, here were two men telling each other what they had been through, with no judgments and no preaching. It was the answer many of us would need.

June 10, 1935, the day Dr. Bob had his last drink, is the day we celebrate the founding of AA.

Eventually the American Medical Association would give Alcoholics Anonymous credit for solving a problem doctors had not been able to solve with prescriptions and lectures. They came to honor Alcoholics Anonymous for saving lives, and giving back to alcoholics their respect, their health, and their ability to live in the world without drinking.

Bob Smith and Bill Wilson had little in common other than alcoholism. Smith was a well-known proctologist in Akron, whose long and successful practice had been deteriorating since his decline into alcoholism, and St. Michael Hospital, where he practiced, was refusing to let him operate. His hands shook, he was unable to show up for appointments, and his wife and friends were beside themselves with worry over his health. Smith was also a member of the Oxford Group and his fellow members had been praying for something, someone, to help their friend with his drinking. They were hoping for a miracle.

Smith and Wilson spent the days following their historic talk looking for other drinkers who needed help with their alcoholism. They visited St. Thomas Hospital, where the head nurse, Sister Ignatia, who saw that her friend was a changed man, helped the two men make contact with others who were just out of detox, jittery and frightened, and lead them to sober lives. And among members of the Oxford Group, the two men shared their stories with other drinkers.

Smith and Wilson brought their prospects to Smith's home, where his wife, Anne, helped welcome new members with food and a place to meet and talk. This began the first group of what would later become known as Alcoholics Anonymous.

Wilson eventually brought the new approach back to New York where he began talking to alcoholics in the Oxford Group and helping many of them find sobriety. He and his group of alcoholics added another six steps to the Oxford Group's original six, enlarging their spiritual grip on the minds of alcoholics.

THE TWELVE STEPS OF ALCOHOLICS ANONYMOUS

1. We admitted we were powerless over alcohol—
   that our lives had become unmanageable.

2. Came to believe that a Power greater than ourselves could restore us to sanity.

3. Made a decision to turn our will and our lives over to the care of God AS WE UNDERSTOOD HIM.

4. Made a searching and fearless moral inventory of ourselves.

5. Admitted to God, to ourselves, and to another human being the exact nature of our wrongs.

6. Were entirely ready to have God remove all these defects of character.

7. Humbly asked Him to remove our shortcomings.

8. Made a list of all persons we had harmed, and became willing to make amends to them all.

9. Made direct amends to such people wherever possible, except when to do so would injure them or others.

10. Continued to take personal inventory and when we were wrong promptly admitted it.

11. Sought through prayer and meditation to improve our conscious contact with God AS WE UNDERSTOOD HIM, praying only for knowledge of His will for us and the power to carry that out.

12. Having had a spiritual awakening as the result of these steps, we tried to carry this message to alcoholics, and to practice these principles in all our affairs.

One of the people who helped Wilson with his spiritual recovery was Father Ed Dowling. They met at the Oxford Group meetings at Calvary Church. Dowling spoke with Wilson about many of the problems that came up during the founding of AA. He was also overweight and desperate to overcome his addiction to food. He would tell Wilson that he had the same problem with food that Wilson and his friends had with booze. The comment drew no immediate responses from Wilson, who did not have a problem with food; if anything, he had a problem eating enough. However, later in the history of AA, the idea was discussed at one of the international conferences that a group called Fatties Anonymous should probably be started to help people like Dowling. His comment remains in the annals of AA, a watchword for those who would come to trust the twelve steps for any addiction as surely as those who used AA to stop drinking.

At first AA was all men. When the groups were four years old, Marty Mann became the first female member in 1939. Over the next eighty years, AA groups have continued to grow and can now be found in cities around the world, with more than two million meetings and an estimated ten million recovering addicts.

Since the first meetings of AA, other groups were formed so that today those who wish to find a way out of other addictions can find plenty of company in their journey. Anonymous programs using the AA literature and twelve steps include those to help people with a multitude of addictions—addictions to grains and sugar, gambling and sex, rage and drugs, and many other overweening and debilitating problems. The meetings are free to all, and the original steps made it clear that everyone and anyone can qualify to join these Anonymous groups of recovering addicts.

In 1959 Rozanne S., a compulsive overeater who was desperate for a solution to her food issues, saw a report on TV about a recovery program called Gamblers Anonymous. Rozanne and her husband, Marvin, had a friend who was suffering from a gambling addiction. They decided to take him to a meeting to see if he could find some help. Sitting at the meeting, listening to the stories of people whose lives had nearly been ruined by their addiction to gambling and who had found relief and healing in GA, Rozanne realized this was what she needed in her life. She could see that her eating habits were not a sign of a moral lack but were part of an illness. It took her a year to put all the tools together to start the new meeting. At first she tried to rewrite the steps of AA for overeaters, but she decided the twelve steps in AA *would work for any addiction one might have.* The universality in the wording, the fact that no religion is mentioned, that a God of one's choice is sought, and that all are welcome were included in the original twelve steps and would work for food too.

Rozanne came to be known as the "Hungry Housewife."

These are spiritual programs without religious boundaries. All are welcome to attend. No fees or dues, only contributions, but if you cannot donate, just keep coming back. We need *you* more than we need your money.

On January 19, 1960, Rozanne and two friends held the first meeting of Overeaters Anonymous. Eventually the program evolved and a pamphlet was prepared by the board of directors of OA that included the seven suggested plans for eating abstinently. The first plan was the GreySheet (so called because it was printed on gray paper). It included only the foods—protein, fruit, vegetables, and salads—that would stop the cravings cold. Three meals a day, weighed and measured, nothing in between. Healthy, healing, and plentiful, and it works.

Today there are programs for people who suffer from nearly any addictive issue, including Compulsive Eaters Anonymous (CEA–HOW), Food Addicts in Recovery Anonymous (FA), Food Addicts Anonymous (FAA), and GreySheeters Anonymous (GSA). In addition, Anorexics and Bulimics Anonymous (ABA) is there for those who suffer from undereating and purging.

Anorexia and bulimia, morbid obesity, and overindulgence in sugar and flour have driven overweight people and people with a food fixation into institutions and pushed them to follow fad diets. They have been shoved aside and told they are weak, or have no backbone, no willpower. Food addicts carry around the evidence on their bodies or in their behavior: not eating at all, eating everything in sight and then throwing it up; taking every pill they can think of to stop the cravings; becoming rail thin or gaining a hundred or more pounds.

Since the advent of modern diets, people have been getting some kind of help, certainly more help than the alcoholic in the years before 1935 when Wilson and Smith founded Alcoholics Anonymous. The Anonymous programs that found their way to overeaters, bulimics, anorexics, and dangerously obese people are there as a guide to recovery. In that regard, the founders of Anonymous groups for other addictions have joined our collection of diet gurus, and have given us help in overcoming many destructive, life-threatening addictions.

We are all in the same lifeboat, but the rescue ship is in the harbor, and we can all come aboard.

CHAPTER 22

MY JOURNEY

The Solution—Celebration

> Calm mind brings inner strength and self-confidence, so
> that's very important for good health.
>
> —DALAI LAMA

Today I use food to treat my eating disorder. And because
I eat only food that does not lead to cravings, I have no
cravings.

Hallelujah! My mind is clear, my heart is light, my
health is perfect.

I have had many years of recovery from compulsive
overeating since I got sober and joined the Anonymous
food program in 1982, and on which I became abstinent from bulimia. There were some changes in the food
plan that my original program proposed, and I did gain
some weight and fall into some old habits, though I never
binged again and always attended meetings.

In 2008 I discovered once again the original plan that had made such a difference in my life. Now I attend GreySheeters Anonymous and follow its very clear plan of abundant, delicious, satisfying, and healthy meals. It worked for me in the beginning and has continued to work for me. I surrendered to it and never looked back. The food no longer talks to me. I eat bountifully.

I bought digital scales and use them to eat three weighed and measured meals a day. Mental clarity and peace of mind finally came with a greater vision of what comes with weight loss in combination with the great program that Bill Wilson and Dr. Bob Smith formulated so many decades ago. Today the energy level I have is amazing, even to me. Recovery began with a simple plan, an adherence to the way of life that was given to me in the Anonymous programs, and an overall sense of joy. I eat only three meals a day, and I do not snack—not on holidays, not at night, not between meals, not when it is Saturday.

I believe I have found a fountain of youth.

There is no deprivation, just health and pleasure and the path to a different kind of life. With this food plan you will find in a few days—sooner sometimes—that you have absolutely no cravings. This is scientific, when you come right down to it. Most diets call for the removal of trigger foods—sugar, wheat, flour, grains, and junk. That is usually in the first thirty days, when you feel fantastic and have already started dropping weight—some people will lose ten to twenty pounds in this first phase. I am saying, "Stay here. Do not go back to the old way." When my diet gurus or my doctor or my close friend or my own addiction starts saying, "Now you are ready to add back the foods that were killing you"—I don't do it.

The old way for many of us, after we got rid of the fat on some crash diet, or even one that seemed sane and took off the pounds slowly but surely, was to think, "Now I can do it my way again," stopping at the local doughnut shop, snacking at parties, having a pick-me-up at eleven and another at four, eating all of the food on our plate at a restaurant. I do whatever I have to do to stay abstinent. My food plan is very simple.

This plan comes with a spiritual program, sharing friends who are doing what I am doing, calling or e-mailing my sponsor my food list on a daily basis. I am now sober for thirty-nine years. I have been in recovery from bulimia for more than thirty-three years. I go to Anonymous food meetings. Sometimes I will take backup food if I am going to a dinner party and add it to my plate, or wait till I get home if I can't get what I want. I do not take chances when I go out to eat but ask for an extra plate to weigh my food when I need it. I do this quietly, and give the waiter a couple of dollars for helping me. I always try to bring my digital scale when I go out to dinner. I have one scale for my kitchen, one for my purse, one for the car, two for long trips. I am not perfect at all of this, but I give it my best shot. Weighing in public may be the most important thing I do. Anyone who pays much attention to this small but powerful act sees recovery in practice and may need the message we carry into the world. It may seem offensive to them. That might be a very good thing.

I am on planes a couple of hundred times a year. I pack my lunch and dinner if I am going to need it, and a hostage meal to carry on the plane. In my checked luggage is a cooler bag with proteins, veggies, salads, fruit, some of it weighed out in servings. Most hotels will put a small refrigerator in your room or will keep your food in a refrigerator in their kitchen. Don't use the minibar cooler, which is not really cold enough for food. Sometimes if there is no fridge I just put a couple of bags of ice in my insulated food bag, which does the trick overnight.

Yogurt and fruit are easy for breakfast. I usually include a jar of soy nut butter, which does not need refrigeration, along with salt, pepper, sweetener, napkins, forks, knives—everything to have a pleasant meal, including a pretty bowl and a beautiful cup for my coffee.

And yes, I am still addicted to caffeine! There was a time when I would go through two or three pots of Zabar's best espresso, ground fresh from those fragrant six-foot-tall woven bags in the store on Broadway. Now I have about three and a half cups a day; I stopped drinking decaf (which is made with chemicals to which I am allergic) except when I don't have to sing.

Fat-free diets have been prescribed for many years by

doctors. Before getting into recovery for my food addiction, I ate skinny foods—no chicken or turkey skin, no full-fat cheese, only vinegar or mustard or nothing on my salad. I was deprived of one of the main ingredients for losing weight—fat! Who would have guessed? Today I have full-fat cheese, skin on the turkey and chicken, and four tablespoons of fat, oil, salad dressing, and/or butter a day. Wow!

It has become clear that it is corn, wheat, grains, sugar, and junk, *not oil and fat,* that is making us eat more and gain weight. Fat is my friend, and yours, but in measured daily doses. Atkins knew it, Donaldson knew it. Taller knew it.

I call it the "Hallelujah Program" and it is the one for me. Maybe it will bring your "numbers" down when you get tested by your doctor, his astonished reaction at your loss of weight, low blood pressure, and shining eyes. It might just be the thing that will turn your life around too.

Since surrendering to this food plan, I am happier, healthier, more serene, stronger, less apt to have colds and the flu. My doctor says I am in pristine health. My cholesterol is great. No heart problems, good blood pressure. My asthma has been in remission for twenty-three years—due in part to diet and in part to acupuncture, the right minerals, alternative doctors who use noninvasive testing to find what I am allergic to, and a mound of vitamins and minerals.

I believe my food plan is as close to the organic life of my ancient ancestors as I am likely to have. A clarity has come over me since I have started eating what is basically the cuisine of the wild hunter-gatherers. It works for me. And perhaps it will work for you.

I know from years of painful experience that a food illness might not show in the body, but it exists in the mind. The illness was in control until I found a way of peace and tranquillity that did not involve fighting food all day long, every day. What happened to Karen Carpenter was something I can understand. As the truth of Karen's illness has come out over the years, her life as an anorexic, bulimic, faster, and dieter has added to the understanding of just how deadly eating disorders can be.

These are not moral issues; they are illnesses.

I am in my seventies and still do pretty much the same things I have always done. I exercise almost every day, and I do the self-realization meditation taught by the Yogananda Institute. Meditation comes in many forms. There are lots of choices and you can find the one that suits you: swim or walk or observe nature. You can light a candle, spend some quiet time thinking of a favorite prayer or counting your blessings or praying for friends and family, remembering all the while to keep your mind clear. There is Transcendental Meditation and there is yoga, a physical and spiritual form of body and mind unity. But for a wholly satisfying experience, find your own method and enjoy the quiet, the peace, the unity with the universe.

I am working harder in my career than ever—singing, writing, recording albums, performing more than a hundred shows a year. It is a glorious life. It is also a complicated, difficult life. Not everything has been a walk in the park since my release from the foods to which I am allergic. Friends and family members have died, financial and business problems have arisen. And there have been celebrations, for the sobriety of family members and the joy of our great-grandson's birth.

One of the things I know as an alcoholic is that I cannot drink. But three times a day I *have* to eat.

I—like William Banting, William the Conqueror, and Lord Byron, like Karen Carpenter, like Cornaro, like Donaldson and Taller, Atkins and Stillman and Hauser, Tarnower and the paleo diet gurus—have experienced a problem with health. With food. I nearly lost my life, my career, my sanity, my health from drinking and from my eating disorder. I know that the right food is exactly the problem, as well as the solution, to my eating disorder.

Today I am abstinent, free of bulimia, of compulsive overeating, of the insanity of dieting. Today I am happy, joyful, and grateful. I want to suggest to you that if you are at all inconvenienced by your relationship to food, you should find a plan that might help you live with joy around your meals and in your life.

I wish you luck on your journey, and pray that you will find the answers you are seeking. Never stop seeking, they are there, and it is possible to recover from obesity and other kinds of eating disorders. I know, I searched too.

Like Banting, I feel compelled to share at least part of the story of how I got here. May you find the path that will bring you peace and health, clarity and serenity, and the good life you seek.

It may not be the one you imagined. It may be worlds better. You could not have dreamed what will come to you if you let the light in.

Acknowledgments

Thanks to Nan Talese, who published my first memoir, *Trust Your Heart,* in 1987. Nan and her husband, Gay, are an inspiration and a comfort in my life. Thank you for taking on *Cravings*! Aidan Charles Kahn, my nephew, suggested the title in 2014. Doris D. for leading me to recovery from bulimia. Susan Raihoffer, of the David Black Agency, who is my agent and who has worked tirelessly on *Cravings,* before, during, and after the idea came to me. Katherine Hourigan, managing editor at Knopf/Doubleday, who was of enormous help in giving me a wonderful edit on the page, the old-fashioned way. A special thanks to Bette Alexander, editorial production manager, and her team and to my copy editor, Karla Eoff, for all the help in editing *Cravings.* My readers—Louis Nelson, Holly Collins, Jayne Pepper, Julia Cameron, Susan Cheever, MaryPat McDermott, Marjorie Wolfe, Virginia Dwan, Hollis Taylor, Jerry Mundis, and Ron

Chernow. Thank you! Sheila Weller, for your encouraging words and brilliant insights.

Thanks to Carolyn Williams, assistant to Nan Talese and of great help in every way; Emily Mahon, for the amazing jacket design; Judy Jacoby, wonderfully imaginative in marketing and all that entails; Todd Doughty, with that beautiful smile, who is in charge of publicity; Rachel Epp, my assistant at Rocky Mountain Productions; to a former editor of mine who shall remain nameless and who said after he read the first draft of *Cravings,* "If Judy publishes this book it will ruin her life." Thank you! And to Jesse Kornbluth who said that that comment would be a valuable asset to selling the book! Dr. Robert Giller, Dr. Lawrence Caprio, Dr. Richard Ash, and Lydia Hall, who helped me find alternative approaches to healing my asthma and other physically depleting conditions that plagued me, as well as giving me advice on homeopathy and vitamin therapy. Dr. Stanley Gitlow, a medical saint to alcoholics, who sent me to treatment for my alcoholism. All members of twelve-step Anonymous groups who have shared their experience, strength, and hope with me over my decades of recovery.

And to all who read this book, whether they suffer from any of the conditions I speak of here or have just plain had enough of the yo-yo battle with weight, diets, fads, fasting, bingeing, and being miserable about having to eat every day—or perhaps know someone who does.

I mean only to share my experience and hope it helps someone.

Thanks to my loving family and my understanding friends who are always there for me.

Finally, to Katherine De Paul, my manager and major-domo, for all the work on *Cravings* over the years.

And to Louis Nelson, my wonderful husband, who has stood by me through thick and thin (if you will pardon the pun) and understands it all.

Judy's Simple Food Plan

You can find the programs that feature this food plan on the GreySheeters Anonymous website, along with meeting information, telephone numbers, and lists of sponsors. Information is free to all. I only suggest this plan, and do not guarantee that it will do for you what it has done for me; these are suggestions only.

BREAKFAST

- 1 cup of plain yogurt (I love FAGE, but any Greek yogurt is good)
- 1 cup of fruit (pineapple, berries of some kind, or apples will do)
- Coffee

LUNCH

- 4 ounces of protein (sliced chicken, beef, turkey, ham, bacon, or other protein; if I have cheese, I eat 2 ounces instead of 4—I like Jarlsberg, blue, Camembert, feta, and Swiss but no low-fat cheeses or protein)
- 2 cups salad and/or vegetables (steamed, sautéed, or raw)
- 1 tablespoon oil

DINNER

- 4 ounces of protein (if cheese, only 2 ounces)
- 3 cups (24 ounces) salad and/or vegetables (steamed, sautéed, or raw)
- 3 tablespoons of fat (butter, oil, or salad dressing)

I do not eat between meals, no matter what, not even holidays, parties, weddings, or funerals. I do not eat snacks, or junk, or dessert, or sugar. For me it is three meals a day, nothing in between, all weighed and measured, with no sugar, carbs, wheat, grains, or junk.

The foods I eat are the usual suspects—protein of all kinds: beef, fish, chicken, turkey (I am not a vegetarian yet), soy products, including tofu and miso, as well as soy nuts and soy nut butter.

You should discuss vitamins with your health professional, preferably a naturopath, as most Western doctors do not use many vitamins or understand the necessity for them.

I am pretty out there with vitamins, but you can keep it very simple: a multivitamin, an extra powerful B complex, vitamin C, krill oil, and quercitin, which makes it all work. Also, if you have bone loss, as I do, ask your doctor about taking ipriflavone and extra vitamins D and K. Now Solgar and other companies make a D/K combination for the bones.

I avoid bisphosphonates, like Fosamax, and use vitamins and minerals instead. Exercise will also go a long way to strengthening bones. I have a treadmill and a stationary bike in my apartment, and I use one-pound weights when I am on them. Jane Fonda taught that in her early exercise videos, which I have used for years as a cross-training discipline, having memorized the routine so I can do it while I watch TV! I take a balance of:

· Multivitamins
· Glucosamine-sulfate with MSM (for osteoporosis)

- Ipriflavone (again for bone health)
- Calcium
- Vitamin tri-K
- Acidophilus (which helps prevent yeast infections when taking antibiotics, as well as maintaining overall health)
- Ginkgo for memory
- L-lysine (to counteract the virus that causes shingles and herpes)
- DHEA, maca, and turmeric (which is used in Indian cooking but is also said by many health-food experts to be a highly effective antiviral compound)

I also take an adult aspirin against heart attack (since I have had a TIA—a transient ischemic attack, which is known as a "warning stroke"). Please consult your physician about this as you may have a condition that precludes the use of aspirin. And I take three cranberry pills every day to counter vaginal disorders.

Then there is laughter, the best medicine. Read *Born Standing Up* by Steve Martin. Watch videos of Robin Williams and Joan Rivers. Watch John Cleese and your favorite comics. Watch a Victor Borge special!

And, remember, Anonymous meetings are free and can be found all over the world (as well as online and via telephone).

Resources

Alcoholics Anonymous. www.aa.org.

Alcoholics Anonymous. *Alcoholics Anonymous Comes of Age*. New York: Alcoholics Anonymous World Services, 1957.

Banting, William. *Letter on Corpulence*. 1864. Reprinted. Andesite Press, 2013.

Cohen, Jennie. "10 Things You May Not Know About William the Conqueror." Available at http://www.history.com/news /history-lists/10-things-you-may-not-know-about-william-the -conqueror.

Cornaro, Luigi. *The Art of Living Long*. Milwaukee, WI: William F. Butler, 1916.

Davis, Adelle. *Let's Get Well*. New York: Signet, 1988.

Davis, William. *Wheat Belly*. Emmaus, PA: Rodale Books, 2014.

Farrell, Amy Erdman. *Fat Shame*. New York: New York University Press, 2011.

Foxcroft, Louise. *Corsets and Calories*. London: Profile Books, 2012.

———. "Lord Byron: The Celebrity Diet Icon." *BBC News Magazine*, January 3, 2012.

Gaffigan, Jim. *Food: A Love Story*. New York: Crown Publishing Group, 2014.

GreySheeters Anonymous. www.greysheet.org.

Hauser, Gayelord. *The Gayelord Hauser Cookbook*. New York: Coward-McCann, 1946.

———. *Look Younger, Live Longer*. New York: Farrar, Straus and Giroux, 1950.

Lustig, Robert H. *Fat Chance*. New York: Plume, 2014.

McCleary, Larry. *Feed Your Brain, Lose Your Belly*. Austin, TX: Greenleaf Book Group, 2011.

Pauling, Linus. *Vitamin C, the Common Cold, and the Flu*. New York: W. H. Freeman, 1976.

S., Rozanne. *Beyond Our Wildest Dreams*. Rio Rancho, NM: Overeaters Anonymous, 1996.

Seymour, Ashley. *Paleo Diet for Beginners*. Amazon Digital Services, 2014.

Smith, Dr. Bob, and Bill Wilson. *The Big Book of Alcoholics Anonymous*. New York: Alcoholics Anonymous World Services, 1939.

Wadd, William. *Cursory Remarks on Corpulence, or, Obesity Considered as a Disease*. 1816. Reprinted. London: Forgotten Books, 2013.

ABOUT THE AUTHOR

Judy Collins has recorded more than forty albums during her illustrious career. With several top-ten hits, Grammy nominations, and gold- and platinum-selling albums to her credit, she has also written several books and has her own music label, Wildflower Records.

A NOTE ABOUT THE TYPE

This book was set in a version of the well-known Mono-
type face Bembo. This letter was cut for the celebrated
Venetian printer Aldus Manutius by Francesco Griffo, and
first used in Pietro Cardinal Bembo's *De Aetna* of 1495.

The companion italic is an adaptation of the chan-
cery script type designed by the calligrapher and printer
Lodovico degli Arrighi.